Organisational Change and the Psychological Contract

David E. Guest

Neil Conway

David Guest is Professor of Organisational Psychology and Human Resource Management at King's College, London. Prior to joining King's, he was Professor of Occupational Psychology and head of the Department of Organisational Psychology at Birkbeck College for 10 years (1990–2000). He has written and researched extensively in the areas of human resource management, employment relations and the psychological contract, motivation and commitment, and careers. He is a member of the editorial advisory board of a number of journals and a Council Member of the Tavistock Institute. His current research is concerned with the relationship between human resource management and performance; the individualisation of employment relations and the role of the psychological contract; flexibility and employment contracts; and the future of the career.

Neil Conway has been a researcher in the Department of Organisational Psychology at Birkbeck College since 1994, where he completed his PhD in Organisational Psychology in 1998. His main research interests include the psychological contract, human resource management, motivation, organisational citizenship behaviours, absenteeism and contingent work. With David Guest, he was the major contributor to the reports on the 1996, 1997 and 1998 IPD Survey of the Employment Relationship.

The Chartered Institute of Personnel and Development is the leading publisher of books and reports for personnel and training professionals, students, and all those concerned with the effective management and development of people at work. For full details of all our titles, please contact the Publishing Department:

Tel: 020 8263 3387
Fax: 020 8263 3850

E-mail: publish@cipd.co.uk

The catalogue of all CIPD titles can be viewed on the CIPD website:
www.cipd.co.uk/publications

Organisational Change and the Psychological Contract

An analysis of the 1999 CIPD Survey

David E. Guest
The Management Centre, King's College, London

Neil Conway
School of Management and Organisational Psychology
Birkbeck College, University of London

First published 2001

Cover design by Curve
Designed and typeset by Beacon GDT
Printed in Great Britain by Short Run Press

British Library Cataloguing in Publication Data
A catalogue record for this book is available from the British Library

ISBN 0 85292 835 1

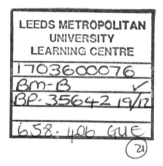

Chartered Institute of Personnel and Development,
CIPD House, Camp Road, London SW19 4UX

Tel: 020 8971 9000
Fax: 020 8263 3333
Website: www.cipd.co.uk

Incorporated by Royal Charter. Registered charity no. 1079797.

The sample

Because the sample is largely drawn from those who provided information in 1998, we shall not go into detail on the organisational context or the sample in the main report. Details of the 1999 sample can be found in the appendices. It is worth noting that the samples in 1998 and this 1999 group are not quite comparable. In the 1998 survey, 92 per cent agreed to be contacted again in the future. Despite assiduous attempts to follow up the 920 who had agreed to be re-interviewed, it proved possible to complete interviews with only 619. Among the rest, most could not be contacted. Several had changed their telephone number or moved home. Some were away from home and some did not have the time to be interviewed. The group most likely to be under-represented are younger men in blue-collar jobs. This should be borne in mind in what follows.

Among the 619 who were re-interviewed, 493 were in the same job with the same organisation as a year ago; 37 were not in employment; 60 had moved to a different organisation. The remaining 29 had moved to a different part of the same organisation. In addition, a number, more particularly among those on temporary and fixed-term contracts, had changed their contractual status.

The next chapter, presenting the main results for 1999, looks just at the 493 who are doing the same job with the same organisation. This provides a more rigorous basis for the analysis of the impact of changes in policy and practice. Chapter 3 looks more closely at those who have changed jobs or employment status.

Contents

Foreword

The CIPD and the psychological contract

When the CIPD first engaged with the idea of the psychological contract some five years ago, few people in the UK – whether academics or practitioners – could see much value in it. Since then, a series of annual surveys of employee attitudes undertaken by the CIPD has helped to build a more robust picture of what the psychological contract is and how it works. Increasing numbers of practitioners now see it as a useful tool that can offer practical help in deciding how to handle issues arising within the employment relationship.

This report by Professor David Guest and Dr Neil Conway breaks new ground by exploring the attitudes of people who had also participated in the previous year's survey. This means they have been able to take into account changes over time and reinforce the evidence showing that the psychological contract is a key influence on employee commitment. The results also confirm that giving employees the opportunity to participate directly in managing their work will produce higher commitment, while long working hours will tend to reduce it. These statements are not simply assertions, but are based on sound evidence.

The impact of workplace change

The main focus of this study was, however, employees' experience of change. It is accepted that change is the only constant in today's workplaces. Predictably one in two employees in the survey reported that their organisation had been going through a major change programme over the past year. In many cases these changes included mergers and acquisitions, redundancies, restructuring and workplace reorganisation.

Not all change is painful: it depends on the nature and scale of change. Increased work responsibilities, or changes in technology, are generally reported as positive rather than negative. In general the report concludes that change has become a normal, accepted and often positive part of life at work.

The scale of change makes a difference. Where large amounts of change have been occurring, workers feel less secure, less motivated and less satisfied with life as a whole. Looking at different types of change, redundancy programmes stand out as having particularly negative effects, and the report gives a strong signal that 'organisations should avoid redundancy programmes if at all possible'. Similarly, changes affecting how, when and where work is carried out are shown to have a strongly negative impact on both employment relations and job security, and the report suggests that 'changes in personnel policy should not be entered into lightly'.

Contract violation

One problem some practitioners had with the model of the psychological contract when they first became aware of it was a reluctance to accept that employers should be 'punished' for unintended breaches of the contract. Why should managers have to accept the downside of low levels of employee commitment when this was due to circumstances beyond their own control?

Fortunately for managers' own sense of fair play, the research finds that employees *do* distinguish between different kinds of contract violation or breach, according to how far they believe managers are to blame. In general terms, employees believe that managers are culpable in about 50 per cent of all cases where they perceive the contract has been breached – mostly where they see this as due to incompetence or a deliberate intention to mislead staff. The emotions aroused when management is held to be responsible for failing to fulfil its side of the deal can be strongly negative. Where management is seen to be not in control, or suffering from heavy pressure or workload, employees are more willing to let it off the hook.

Even where change is seen to be due to external circumstances – as for example in the case of redundancies brought about by loss of market share – damage to the psychological contract may still be considerable. Management may not get the blame, but employees can become demotivated and dissatisfied so the business may still be affected. This reinforces the doubts that have been expressed about the benefits of downsizing and restructuring, particularly where employers adopt this strategy at least partly as a way of demonstrating that management is prepared to be tough on costs.

Who changes jobs?

The report also offers some useful insights into why people change jobs. The report shows that most people who changed their employer in the previous 12 months had done so in order to get away from their existing job. Of these, one in three said they left to improve their pay or prospects; while another one in three found the job too easy or saw no scope for development. Most of the remainder left because either the hours or location were inconvenient, with just one in six moving because they had been offered a better job. The implication is that employee involvement in job design and working patterns might pay off handsomely.

Managers will note that, as governments are said to lose elections rather than oppositions win them, so employees change jobs because they are unhappy rather than because they are positively looking for something better. In other words, managers have more influence over labour turnover than many believe. Predictably, employees who changed jobs had earlier reported lower commitment, lower satisfaction, poorer employment relations, poorer life satisfaction, lower job security and lower motivation. In all, three out of four of those who changed organisations did so from their own choice, no doubt reflecting in part the number of labour market opportunities available.

Human resource practices

One particular finding is somewhat troubling: the report finds a modest decline in the reported use of human resource practices, particularly those aimed at getting people more involved in workplace decision-making and in the scope for direct participation by employees in day-to-day work. What has been going on? The changes are not all one-way: more employees report that their organisation has a 'no compulsory redundancies' policy. But the implication seems to be that we cannot assume steady growth in the use of enlightened practices by employers. The evidence from studies such as that by the Institute of Work Performance at Sheffield University about the impact of people management practices (including involvement) on business performance needs to become more widely known and reinforced by further work.

Mike Emmott

Adviser, Employee Relations
Chartered Institute of Personnel and Development

Executive summary

- This is the fifth CIPD annual survey of the state of the employment relationship. Like the others, the core of the analysis is built around the concept of the psychological contract that captures the individual level at which much of employment relations now takes place. However, it is distinctly different from previous surveys in following up 619 of the nationally representative sample of 1,000 workers who had been interviewed for the previous survey in 1998. Most of the remainder could not be contacted and a minority were unwilling to be re-interviewed. The 1999 study focuses in particular on the subject of change at work.

- Of the 619 we were able to contact, 6 per cent had left employment in the past year, almost 10 per cent had changed employer and just under 5 per cent had moved jobs while staying in the same organisation. The remainder were doing more or less the same job with the same employer.

- Among the 493 in the same jobs, there was a modest decline in the reported use by their employer of human resource practices. This was most apparent with respect to use of quality improvement and employee involvement practices and use of the internal labour market to fill management vacancies. There was also a decline in the scope for direct participation in day-to-day work.

- Working hours are still on the increase: 15 per cent say they have gone up over the past year compared with 8 per cent who say they have gone down. Nevertheless, the proportion saying they have the right balance between work and the rest of life has gone up from 75 per cent to 78 per cent over the year. Longest hours are worked by senior managers with high incomes who are also most likely to report a poor balance between work and life outside work. They admit that when the two spheres of life are in conflict, work invariably wins.

- After improving between 1996 and 1998, employee responses, reflected in attitudes and behaviour, have declined slightly between 1998 and 1999. The decline is stronger in the areas of motivation and willingness to work outside the prescribed role. Some of this decline can be attributed to the reduced application of human resource practices and direct participation.

- Despite the decline in attitudes and behaviour, most workers remain generally satisfied and secure, highly motivated and provide a broadly positive account of the experience of work.

- A positive psychological contract in 1998 was a good predictor of an increase in work satisfaction, commitment, job security, employment relations and reduced intention to change employment between 1998 and 1999. Human resource practices and direct participation have a strong influence on the state of the psychological contract.

- Human resource practices in 1998 and in 1999 are a good predictor of self-rated improvement in performance between 1998 and 1999.

- Most of those who moved jobs during the year say they chose to move and most are now more satisfied and motivated and report that the move was a positive step.

- 49 per cent reported that some form of organisational change had taken place in the previous year. Where large numbers of changes had occurred, this tended to have a damaging impact on motivation and on attitudes such as satisfaction, commitment and job security.

- The type of change had an impact on reactions. Redundancy programmes invariably had a negative impact on the attitudes of workers who remained, while technological change had a positive impact on both attitudes and behaviour.

- A majority of workers reported some sort of workplace change in the previous year, mainly affecting the design and organisation of work or the technology and the products/services. A change of boss affected 29 per cent, and 34 per cent reported changes in their job content. In each case, between two-thirds and three-quarters said the changes resulted in improvements.

- Changes in personnel policies were reported by 22 per cent. These were more likely to have a negative impact, especially those affecting how, when and where work was carried out. Such changes damaged job security and employment relations.

- It was agreed by 38 per cent that there was too much change going on where they worked. On the other hand, 61 per cent disagreed and 61 per cent also believed that changes at work made things better rather than worse. In short, a majority had a positive view of change at work.

- The survey asked whether staff had had their psychological contract violated during the past year. Only 12 per cent reported a serious violation. They usually blamed senior or line management for this. Where, as was quite often the case, this was attributed to either incompetence or deceit, it led to strong negative emotions of anger and betrayal.

- Workers are reluctant to admit that they seriously violate their side of the psychological contract. While large numbers admitted to criticising their employer or managers and to considering other employment from time to time, few would admit to activities that had jeopardised their work performance.

- The general findings of the survey, based on information collected over two years, confirm the importance of the model linking human resource practices to the state of the psychological contract and then, in turn, to attitudes and behaviour. The implication is that policies to apply human resource practices will pay off.

- The reduced levels of application of both human resource practices and direct participation are already beginning to have a negative impact on attitudes and behaviour and are likely to have consequences for organisational performance.

- The findings challenge assumptions about the damaging consequences of change at work. Most workers have positive attitudes towards change and most believe that changes they have experienced have had positive outcomes. The exceptions are personnel-related changes, often at organisational level, that communicate negative signals. These include in particular redundancy programmes and imposed changes in working arrangements.

- Where workers feel they have some control over the changes, they are generally positive and feel that such changes benefit both individual and organisation. Again there are clear policy implications about what sort of changes are likely to be more or less well received and about how the process of change might be effectively managed.

1 | Introduction

◘ **The impact that change at work is said to have on employee–management relations is one of the main reasons for the burgeoning interest in the psychological contract.**

◘ **The amount of change and general turbulence at work opens up the prospect of more contract violation, as promises made in apparent good faith can no longer be kept.**

Change is a dominant theme of modern working life and it forms the focus of this year's CIPD report on the psychological contract and the state of the employment relationship in Britain. It is all too easy to write in clichés about change. It is both an opportunity and a threat. There is a constant refrain that there is too much change. There is certainly a temptation on the part of new governments and new managers to introduce wholesale changes, often – it might appear to those on the receiving end – without sound justification for the disruption caused. Not surprisingly, employees grow somewhat cynical about such change. Commitment to a specific change remains conditional in the sure knowledge that it will soon be overtaken by further changes.

The more serious side of change, from the workers' perspective, is that too much change can be a major source of stress and unhappiness. This may be more likely to occur where people feel that they have no control over the changes that affect them. This brings us into the realm of people management and the psychological contract. Clearly the process of change can have an impact on the outcomes. Furthermore, if people feel cheated or misled by management-initiated change, then their relationship with their employer – their psychological contract – will deteriorate. Indeed, one of the reasons for the resurgence of interest in the psychological contract is a belief that the nature of the relationship between the individual and the organisation has been changing.

First of all, the old 'deal', whether it be a fair day's work for a fair day's pay or a predictable organisational career in return for loyalty, appears to be breaking down. Second, the amount of change and general turbulence at work opens up the prospect of more contract violation as promises made in apparent good faith can no longer be kept. This can have damaging consequences for both individual and organisation.

The headlines tend to highlight the negative aspects of change. More balanced views see both the positive as well as the negative; while Britain is losing some old car plants, inward investment remains as buoyant as ever. Also, balanced views will set continuity alongside change. Thus, while job change appears to be ever more common, an underlying continuity reveals that the average tenure in a job has changed only slightly during the past 20 years or more. All this raises questions about whether it is the idea of change or the experience of change that constitutes the apparent threat and whether people really believe that they personally are affected by too much change. This can be translated into a number of specific questions. Among those who experience change, does it leave them feeling better or worse off? What impact does it have on family life and on the balance between work and the rest of life? Do good human resource practices affect the reaction to change? In particular, does the experience of involvement in change affect reactions to the change? In this context, what role do trade unions

> ' ... one of the reasons for the resurgence of interest in the psychological contract is a belief that the nature of the relationship between the individual and the organisation has been changing.'

play in change? And, are those affected by change really more likely to feel that their relationship with the organisation – their psychological contract – has been violated?

These are some of the issues that are explored in the 1999 CIPD survey. The survey is distinctive in its sample. It consists of a follow-up of those who were interviewed for the 1998 report, most of whom had agreed in 1998 to be re-interviewed. The report has three distinct parts. The first is an analysis of findings for the 1999 sample, at the same time providing, where possible, an analysis of any changes since 1998. It also contains an analysis of the longitudinal element; in other words, an attempt to explore how far attitudes and experiences reported in 1998 predict outcomes in 1999. This allows us to make more confident claims about cause and effect than is the case with a survey from a single year. The report

then examines in more detail the experience of change, considering who is affected by it, how, and with what effect. This forms two chapters looking first at the experience of job change and second at various aspects of organisational change. The final chapter of results looks in more detail at violation of the psychological contract, since this is a recurring theme in the popular analysis of change at work. It allows us to make some assessment, discussed in the concluding chapter, of how far the experience of change at work is considered to be a problem by those whom it affects.

The conceptual framework

As in previous reports, we start out with the established conceptual framework set out in Figure 1. However, this year it has been modified to take account of the focus on change.

Figure 1 | The conceptual framework

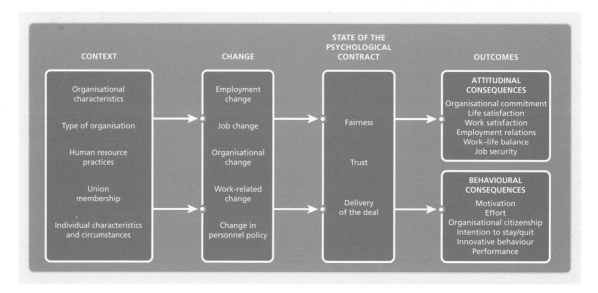

2 | The state of the psychological contract and the employment relationship in 1999

◘ **There has been a decline in employee involvement and quality practices between 1998 and 1999.**

◘ **Despite the evidence linking human resource management and performance, the number reporting that they experience more than half of the list of human resource practices has declined.**

◘ **The state of the psychological contract really matters for workers. It is the key predictor of changes in levels of job satisfaction and organisational commitment between 1998 and 1999.**

◘ **Satisfaction with most aspects of life is high and, if anything, has risen over the year.**

◘ **The number of people trying to move job increased between 1998 and 1999, perhaps reflecting the encouraging state of the labour market.**

In this chapter we present the full results for 1999 and compare them with those for 1998 for the 493 who were employed in the same job in the same organisation. This provides the most rigorous comparison. (Those who have changed employment status are considered in the next chapter.) After describing the results, we shall examine the factors explaining variations in practices, attitudes and behaviour. The longitudinal data – the information from 1998 and 1999 using the same sample with the same questions – allows us to be much more confident about making causal assumptions. We shall develop the analysis of the impact of change on attitudes and behaviour in Chapter 4. This chapter starts with an analysis of practices, specifically human resource practices and direct participation, then moves on to examine the state of the psychological contract, attitudes to work and life as a whole, and work-related behaviour.

Human resource practices

One of the core elements in the analysis in each of the years when we have conducted this survey is an assessment of the relationship between employees' perceptions of human resource practices and their psychological contract. A standard set of 10 questions have been asked in each of the previous three surveys. This year we can make a direct assessment of any changes by comparing the 1999 responses of the 493 in the sample who are currently employed in the same jobs with their responses in 1998. The results are presented in Table 1. This shows the percentage who gave a positive response; in other words, they agreed with the statement. Some of the others may have given a 'don't know' answer rather than a clear negative response.

Table 1 | Experience of human resource practices in 1998 and 1999

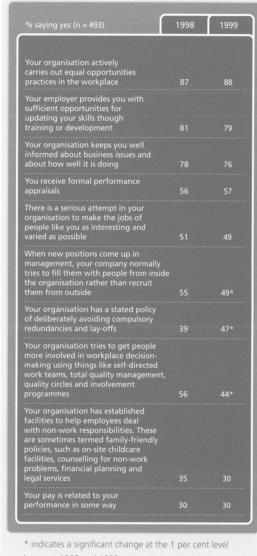

% saying yes (n = 493)	1998	1999
Your organisation actively carries out equal opportunities practices in the workplace	87	88
Your employer provides you with sufficient opportunities for updating your skills though training or development	81	79
Your organisation keeps you well informed about business issues and about how well it is doing	78	76
You receive formal performance appraisals	56	57
There is a serious attempt in your organisation to make the jobs of people like you as interesting and varied as possible	51	49
When new positions come up in management, your company normally tries to fill them with people from inside the organisation rather than recruit them from outside	55	49*
Your organisation has a stated policy of deliberately avoiding compulsory redundancies and lay-offs	39	47*
Your organisation tries to get people more involved in workplace decision-making using things like self-directed work teams, total quality management, quality circles and involvement programmes	56	44*
Your organisation has established facilities to help employees deal with non-work responsibilities. These are sometimes termed family-friendly policies, such as on-site childcare facilities, counselling for non-work problems, financial planning and legal services	35	30
Your pay is related to your performance in some way	30	30

* indicates a significant change at the 1 per cent level between 1998 and 1999.

We might expect either a reasonable stability of response or a slight increase in the use of human resource practices as organisations become more aware of their potential benefits. This does not appear to have occurred. Most items show a modest decline and in some cases a more marked drop. This is particularly the case with respect to the use of quality and employee involvement practices. This appears to contradict the information provided by managers in the 1998 Workplace Employee Relations Survey (Cully *et al*, 1999) but it does fit with the responses of workers in that survey. It may be that these practices are no longer as fashionable as they were. There is also a significant and unexplained reduction in the use of internal promotions to fill management vacancies rather than using the external labour market. This is somewhat puzzling given the tight labour market. On the other hand, there is a significant increase in the reported adoption of redundancy-avoidance policies.

Taken as a whole, the proportion reporting that they experience more than half the human resource practices in their workplace has fallen from a little over 57 per cent in 1998 to 49 per cent in 1999. This change is statistically significant and reflects what some might consider to be a worrying trend bearing in mind that the 1998 survey reported no increase in practices compared with the previous year.

We know from previous surveys something about the organisational and individual background characteristics associated with greater experience of human resource practices. For example, in the 1998 survey, more human resource practices are reported by: those working in both larger organisations and larger establishments; those with a higher income and at more senior management levels; those in white-collar as opposed to blue-collar jobs; and trade union members. There are plausible reasons why all of these background factors influence the use and experience of human resource practices and it is likely that they had a similar influence in 1999. However, none of these characteristics, nor indeed any other background factors, has a significant influence in explaining any *changes* between 1998 and 1999 in the reported number of human resource practices experienced by this sample of workers. This may be because the changes themselves are relatively small and inconsistent.

Direct participation

Four items in the survey ask about the scope for direct participation in day-to-day work. These are included because in previous surveys they have served as a useful measure of one important dimension of organisational climate. But they are also of interest in their own right. The results for the matched sample in 1998 and 1999 are shown in Table 2.

The results across these four direct participation items in Table 2 reveal a consistent decline. It is impossible to determine whether the responses reflect a perceived or real drop in the scope for employees to determine their day-to-day work, but they do mirror the decline in the use of quality and employee involvement practices. Either way, what is revealed is a statistically significant drop in the overall measure of direct participation between 1998 and 1999.

Analysis of influences on this change reveals some interesting patterns. We should start by looking back to the 1998 results. These showed that experience of direct participation was higher among those at more senior levels of management, those on higher incomes and those with a higher level of education. While these may be related, each exerted an independent influence and largely reflects the fact that those in senior posts and in some professional jobs have more control over decisions affecting their work. Direct participation was also higher among those working in smaller organisations and among women, but lower among those in blue-collar jobs. When we look at background factors that explain change between 1998 and 1999 in the

Table 2 | Experience of direct participation

% (n = 493)	Most of the time		Some of the time		Rarely		Never	
	1998	1999	1998	1999	1998	1999	1998	1999
I plan my own work	59	53	19	19	6	10	17	18
I carry out my work in the way I think best	86	83	11	8	1	5	1	3
I vary how I do my work	43	36	33	32	11	17	13	15
I choose the job assignments I work on	24	21	22	21	17	18	36	39

Note: Numbers are rounded and will therefore not always sum to 100 per cent.

> ' ... those who already had high levels of direct control and participation have by and large maintained this, while among those who had less control, it has reduced still further.'

level of direct participation, we find that it is likely to have decreased significantly more among middle managers and blue-collar workers than among those in more senior-level management jobs and those with a higher income. What this implies is that those who already had high levels of direct control and participation have by and large maintained this, while among those who had less control, it has reduced still further. This would not appear to be good news for advocates of partnership at work.

The state of the psychological contract in 1999

In this as in previous surveys, a measure of the state of the psychological contract lies at the heart of the analysis. The state of the psychological contract was measured using three dimensions, namely the extent to which management has kept its promises – the delivery of 'the deal' – and perceived levels of trust and fairness. In 1998 we examined what promises workers believed the organisation had made to them, covering some of

the issues generally agreed to be central to debates about the changing nature of the psychological contract. The analysis found that workers believed that promises were most clearly made with respect to fair treatment at work, reasonable job security and fair pay for the work done. They were rather less likely to be made with respect to providing help outside work, interesting work and a career. Since we would not expect much change in the promises made, in 1999 we focused just on the delivery of promises. Again it is possible to make comparisons with 1998 and the results for the two years are shown in Table 3. The results exclude those who said that no promise had been made to them on a specific item.

These results show a surprising level of variation from one year to the next. Part of this variation may be accounted for by the absence in 1999 of the filter question asking whether any promises had been made. Instead we provided this as one of the possible responses in addition to those listed in Table 3. However, this can account for only part of the variation. In general terms, the

Table 3 | Delivery of promises in the psychological contract in 1998 and 1999

% (n = 493)	Always kept them		Kept them to a large extent		Kept them to some extent		Not kept them at all	
The promise:	1998	1999	1998	1999	1998	1999	1998	1999
To provide you with a reasonably secure job	34	46	43	34	22	17	1	3
To provide you with fair pay for the work that you do	29	40	43	26	26	25	1	8
To provide you with a career	29	42	41	32	28	18	2	8
To provide you with interesting work	31	33	40	28	27	32	1	6
To ensure fair treatment by managers and supervisors	30	38	40	35	28	21	2	5
To help you deal with problems you encounter outside work	29	29	32	30	36	30	3	11

Note: Numbers are rounded and will therefore not always sum to 100 per cent.

responses have become more extreme, with more people believing that promises are kept in full and more indicating that they are not kept at all.

A detailed comparison reveals quite a high degree of volatility in response from one year to the next. It seems that perceptions of the extent to which the organisation keeps its promises are not as stable from year to year as we had initially expected and may well reflect fairly recent experiences and incidents. Stability of individual views, reflected in the proportion giving the same response each year, appears to be greatest with respect to promises concerning interesting work and job security, perhaps because these (and more particularly job security) are relatively long-term issues that may not have been challenged during the year. In contrast, there is most volatility around promises about careers and support outside work. Again we can only speculate, but careers are an emotive issue and responses may reflect short-term feelings of optimism or pessimism, while support outside work may be an issue on which

there is considerable uncertainty about how the organisation might behave. Indeed, the recent higher profile given to family-friendly policies may have raised awareness of company practice. This might also explain the decline in the reported use of family-friendly practices, reported in the earlier section on human resource practices, as workers become more aware of the potential range of such practices. In all this, there is some uncertainty about who or what constitutes the organisation with respect to the psychological contract. This is an issue we are exploring in a separate report.[1]

The other aspects of the state of the psychological contract concern trust and fairness. These were covered by the three core items used in the past. The results and the comparisons with 1998 are shown in Table 4.

The results in Table 4 show a much higher degree of stability than those concerning the delivery of promises. This is reflected in the direct year-on-year comparisons of responses by individuals. Not

Table 4 | Perceptions of fairness and trust in the psychological contract

% (n = 493)	a lot		somewhat		only a little		not at all	
	1998	1999	1998	1999	1998	1999	1998	1999
In general, how much do you trust your organisation to keep its promises or commitments to you and other employees?	32	33	46	50	16	14	6	3
To what extent do you trust management to look after your best interests?	27	27	45	48	19	18	8	7
	yes definitely		yes probably		no probably not		no definitely not	
	1998	1999	1998	1999	1998	1999	1998	1999
Do you feel you are fairly rewarded for the amount of effort you put into your job?	34	27	32	41	17	16	16	16

Note: Numbers are rounded and therefore will not always sum to 100 per cent.

1. Guest D. and Conway N. *Employer Perceptions of the Psychological Contract*. To be published by the CIPD in 2001.

surprisingly, therefore, they reveal no clear pattern of change between 1998 and 1999.

As in previous years, we can combine the three components of the state of the psychological contract – the delivery of promises, trust and fairness – into a single overall measure of the state of the psychological contract. When we do so, we find that there is a significant overall improvement between 1998 and 1999 that can be attributed mainly to the increase in the number of promises that are perceived to be delivered.

We know from previous surveys that a positive psychological contract is consistently associated from year to year with a similar set of background factors. In 1998, the key factors associated with a positive psychological contract were the number of progressive human resource practices in place, a higher salary, scope for direct participation and being on a fixed-term contract. At the same time, a poorer psychological contract was reported by those working in both larger organisations and larger establishments, by those working longer hours and with what they perceived to be the wrong balance between home and work, and by those with longer tenure.

In the present analysis, we are particularly interested in change in the psychological contract between 1998 and 1999. We can start by looking at the range of background factors collected in 1998, including human resource practices and the climate of direct participation. Two factors had a clearly significant impact on changes in the state of the psychological contract; these were tenure and being on a temporary contract, both of which were associated with an improvement, while working hours had a marginally significant negative effect. A number of those on temporary contracts in 1998 will have gained permanent

contracts by 1999, which may explain their improved psychological contract. Tenure is harder to explain. In 1998, longer tenure was associated with a poorer psychological contract but this reverses over time, possibly because those with a poorer psychological contract, as we shall see in Chapter 3, may have moved on and have therefore been excluded from this analysis. Long working hours have both an immediate and a long-term negative effect on the psychological contract. By implication a significant number of those working long hours feel that they are being unreasonably exploited by their organisation.

In noting the volatility of the state of the psychological contract, we suggested that responses might be a reflection of the influence of current concerns. We therefore modified the analysis to explore the influence on change in the psychological contract of current human resource practices and participation climate. This improves our ability to predict the state of the psychological contract. Human resource practices now become highly significant and the scope for direct participation is marginally significant. More of both at the time of the survey in 1999 is associated with an improvement in the psychological contract between 1998 and 1999. Tenure and being on a temporary contract in 1998 also retain their positive influence and longer working hours continue to be associated with a deteriorating psychological contract. In addition, two other factors exert a marginally significant influence. A higher income has a marginal positive influence and working in a larger organisation a marginal negative influence on changes in the psychological contract.

Presenting the results across two years can become quite complicated. Here and in subsequent sections, we shall present a figure

' ... the experience of working in an organisation where more
progressive human resource practices are in place is associated
with an improved state of the psychological contract ... .'

showing the results based on both the 1999
policies, practices and attitudes, which invariably
have the larger influence, and on the 1998
information. The 1998 results present the stronger
test of causal links. The relevant results for the
psychological contract are shown in Figure 2. It is
important to bear in mind in this and in
subsequent figures that they show the factors that
influence *change* in the psychological contract,
whether the change is positive or negative, rather
than the actual level.

One of the key policy implications of these results
is that the experience of working in an
organisation where more progressive human
resource practices are in place is associated with
an improved state of the psychological contract.
The second implication is that the current practices
exert a stronger influence than those in place a
year ago. In other words, while the human
resource practices in place a year ago just fail to
show a significant influence on change in the
psychological contract, the impact of the practices

Figure 2 | Change in the psychological contract

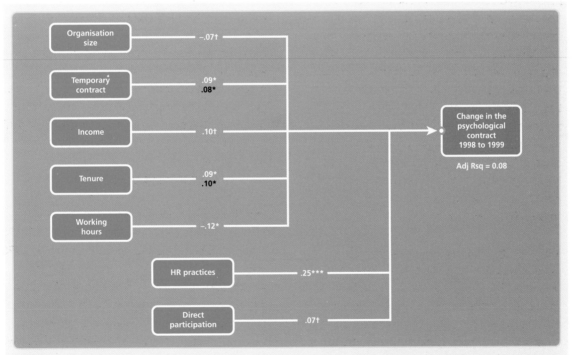

Notes

1   † slightly significant (p<.10); * significant (p<.05); ** strongly significant (p<.01); *** very strongly significant (p<.001). Only significant
    associations are displayed.

2   Black numbers present 1998 associations; white numbers present 1999 associations.

3   The numbers show the beta weights from the regression analysis. A positive score indicates that the variable is associated with an
    improvement in the psychological contract while a negative score reveals that it is associated with a deterioration. The adjusted R-square
    (Adj Rsq) signifies how much variance is explained by the predictors. In this and all subsequent figures, it refers to the 1999 practices and
    attitudes.

in place right now is considerable when we are seeking to explain changes in the state of the psychological contract. The positive influence of tenure suggests that familiarity breeds contentment while the negative impact of working hours is a warning to employers that long hours lead to feelings of inequity and failure to deliver the promised deal.

Attitudes to work

Job satisfaction

There has been recent debate about the level of satisfaction among workers in the UK, with some people suggesting that satisfaction is relatively low. Previous reports in this series have reported a generally high level of job satisfaction and a recent review of other national surveys showed some support for this conclusion (Guest and Conway,

1999). This year we asked two questions, one a repeat of an item used in the previous survey and the other one of the conventional general indicators of job satisfaction. The results are shown in Table 5. The first item is the one asked in both years and is based on responses on a scale from 1 (totally dissatisfied) to 10 (totally satisfied), where 1–3 is scored as low, 4–7 as medium and 8–10 as high work satisfaction.

The results in Table 5 confirm the generally high level of satisfaction, whichever measure is used. While we can debate what proportion of the workforce are highly satisfied, there is strong evidence that only a small proportion are clearly dissatisfied with their work. On the year-to-year comparison, levels of satisfaction have tended to decline a little, though the differences fall just short of statistical significance.

In previous surveys we have shown that higher job satisfaction is associated with a more positive psychological contract, more human resource practices in place, working in smaller organisations, a good balance between home and work, and being older. From this base, we can examine which factors explain *changes* in job satisfaction over the year. Only two factors have a marginally significant predictive influence on changes in job satisfaction between 1998 and 1999; these are the state of the psychological contract in 1998 and age. Higher scores on each predict increased job satisfaction over the year. When we look at current influences on change in job satisfaction, then the state of the psychological contract in 1999 and age both become highly significant, but no other factors exert any influence.

These results confirm that although a range of background factors, including human resource

Table 5 | Job satisfaction

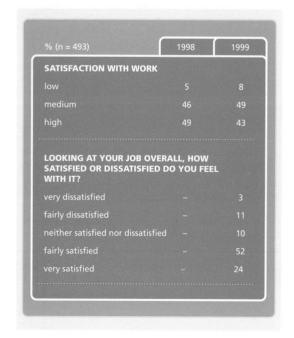

% (n = 493)	1998	1999
SATISFACTION WITH WORK		
low	5	8
medium	46	49
high	49	43
LOOKING AT YOUR JOB OVERALL, HOW SATISFIED OR DISSATISFIED DO YOU FEEL WITH IT?		
very dissatisfied	–	3
fairly dissatisfied	–	11
neither satisfied nor dissatisfied	–	10
fairly satisfied	–	52
very satisfied	–	24

practices, are associated with variations in the level of job satisfaction, among this sample only the state of the psychological contract and age help to explain any changes in job satisfaction and both have a positive influence. By implication, when we are seeking to explain the marginal deterioration in job satisfaction over the year, it seems most likely to have occurred among those who have a poorer psychological contract and who are younger. The results for job satisfaction and for the next item, commitment to the organisation, are shown in Figure 3.

Organisational commitment

The measure of organisational commitment consisted of two items adapted from a larger scale. The same items have been used in previous surveys. The results are shown in Table 6.

Table 6 | Organisational commitment

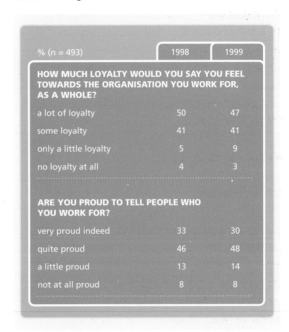

% (n = 493)	1998	1999
HOW MUCH LOYALTY WOULD YOU SAY YOU FEEL TOWARDS THE ORGANISATION YOU WORK FOR, AS A WHOLE?		
a lot of loyalty	50	47
some loyalty	41	41
only a little loyalty	5	9
no loyalty at all	4	3
ARE YOU PROUD TO TELL PEOPLE WHO YOU WORK FOR?		
very proud indeed	33	30
quite proud	46	48
a little proud	13	14
not at all proud	8	8

Figure 3 | Changes in work satisfaction and organisational commitment

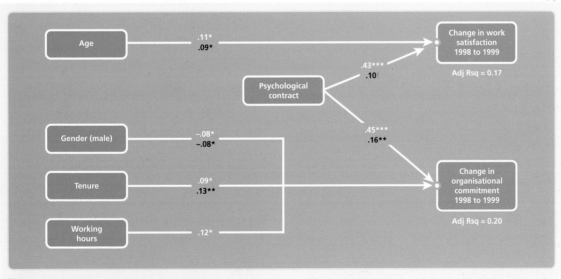

Notes

1   † slightly significant (p<.10); * significant (p<.05); ** strongly significant (p<.01); *** very strongly significant (p<.001). Only significant associations are displayed.

2   Black numbers present 1998 associations; white numbers present 1999 associations.

> **'The results over the past two years confirm that, for most workers, job insecurity is not a matter of great personal concern.'**

The results for organisational commitment show a very slight but insignificant decline, confirming that this is a relatively stable measure.

In previous surveys, the background factors associated with level of commitment are fairly consistent. In 1998, commitment was significantly higher among those with a more positive psychological contract, among those working in smaller organisations, where there were more human resource practices in place, among women and among those with a higher income. It was lower among those in blue-collar jobs. This year we focus on *change* in the level of commitment. Only three factors measured in 1998 predict changes in commitment between 1998 and 1999. These show that commitment was likely to increase over the year among those who reported a positive psychological contract in 1998 and those who had longer tenure. It showed a marginally significant decline among men. If we then look at the influence of current factors, we find that the state of the psychological contract in 1999 becomes the most important influence on changes in commitment to the organisation, while tenure also remains significant. Being male continues to have a marginal negative influence and working hours in 1998 now exert a significant and positive influence on commitment in 1999. This last finding is particularly interesting. It suggests that those who were working long hours in 1998 are likely to have become more committed to the organisation over the year. The implication, supported by other psychological research, is that attitude change may follow behaviour. Leaving this aside, the results show the continuing importance of the state of the psychological contract both in predicting and explaining changes in attitudes to work.

Job security

There has been considerable discussion about levels of job security among the workforce, with some analysts arguing that job insecurity is now rife. Over the years, the CIPD surveys have consistently challenged this view. The results over the past two years confirm that, for most workers, job insecurity is not a matter of great personal concern. The results for our standard question are shown in Table 7.

There is no significant change in levels of reported job security, which remains high. In the 1998 survey, the background factors that had a significant association with a higher level of job security were the state of the psychological contract, having a permanent job as opposed to a temporary or fixed-term contract, being younger, female and in a blue-collar rather than a managerial or professional job.

If we examine the factors that explain changes in level of job security, then the 1998 items that predict change are:

◻ the state of the psychological contract, which is associated with increased job security

Table 7 | Job security

% (n = 493)	1998	1999
HOW SECURE DO YOU FEEL IN YOUR PRESENT JOB?		
very secure	38	36
fairly secure	52	54
fairly insecure	8	8
very insecure	2	2

◻ being on a fixed-term contract, which is associated with reduced job security

◻ working in the public sector, which is associated with increased job security

◻ working in the manufacturing sector, which has a marginally significant impact in predicting decreased job security.

All of these results make sense in terms of what we know about the labour market. When we incorporate the 1999 policy and attitude variables, the explanation of change is stronger but the influences are much the same. The state of the psychological contract and fixed-term contracts retain their influence; so too does working in the public sector. However, working in manufacturing industry ceases to have a significant influence on job security. It is interesting to note that while fixed-term contracts are associated with reduced job security, the same is not true for temporary contracts, possibly, as noted earlier, because many temporary workers have found new, more permanent contracts. We compare the situation of those who were on temporary and fixed-term contracts in the next chapter.

Employment relations

Each year we ask a single general question about the state of relations between employees and management. The results are shown in Table 8.

The results in Table 8 show a small but consistent and statistically significant decline in assessments of the state of employment relations. It is worth noting that 40 per cent of the sample belong to a trade union. This is well above the national figure of about 30 per cent, partly because of the decision to omit smaller organisations as well as the self-employed. Those who belong to a trade union tend to be a little less positive in their assessment of the employment relationship.

We know from previous surveys that the factors associated with the assessment of employee–management relations are consistent over the years. In 1998, the key items associated with a positive assessment were a more positive psychological contract, more human resource management practices, working in smaller establishments and being female. What, then, explains any *change* in the assessment of the employment relationship? Among the factors measured in 1998, which predict changes in employee–management relations between 1998 and 1999? Only the state of the psychological contract has a strong significant influence and it leads to better assessments of employer–employee relations. Being on a temporary contract has a marginally significant positive influence, while working in a larger establishment has a marginally significant negative influence. When we incorporate the 1999 policy and attitude items we explain a higher amount of change. The psychological contract remains a key positive influence but now we find that, contrary to

Table 8 | Employment relations

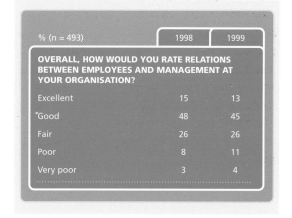

% (n = 493)	1998	1999
OVERALL, HOW WOULD YOU RATE RELATIONS BETWEEN EMPLOYEES AND MANAGEMENT AT YOUR ORGANISATION?		
Excellent	15	13
Good	48	45
Fair	26	26
Poor	8	11
Very poor	3	4

expectations, operating in a climate where there is scope for direct participation is associated with a deterioration in employee–management relations. So too is working in larger establishments. Nothing else has a significant influence.

These results confirm the important link between the psychological contract and employee–manager relations. This is much as we would expect. Why current scope for direct participation is associated with a deterioration in employee–management relations is something of a mystery, unless it reflects dissatisfaction with the reduction in opportunities for direct participation that was noted earlier. The results for the determinants of change in job security and employee–management relations are shown in Figure 4.

Working hours and the balance between home and work life

Work–life balance has become a fashionable topic. It is something we have been asking about each year in this survey. The first important piece of evidence concerns working hours. It has been established that workers in Britain work, on average, longer hours than any of their European counterparts. This year we again asked about the average number of hours worked. The mean was 38.5 hours per week. However, this hides a wide variation, with 17 per cent working 25 hours or less a week, 16 per cent working 40 to 45 hours a week, and 21 per cent working more than 45 hours a week. This includes 97 out of the 493 in the sample who work more than 48 hours a week,

Figure 4 | Changes in job security and employment relations

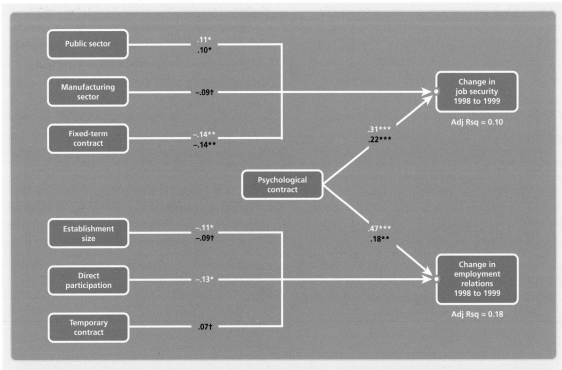

Notes

1 † slightly significant (p<.10); * significant (p<.05); ** strongly significant (p<.01); *** very strongly significant (p<.001). Only significant associations are displayed.

2 Black numbers present 1998 associations; white numbers present 1999 associations.

the cut-off point agreed by the European Union. Indeed, among those working more than 48 hours, the average working week is 54.9 hours. Those working longer hours tend to be the more senior managers.

The trend in working hours still seems to be upwards. While 78 per cent said their hours were about the same as a year ago, 15 per cent said they were more compared with 8 per cent who said they were less. Although we are not discussing them explicitly in this chapter, those who had moved to a different organisation were the most likely to be working fewer hours, while those who had moved to a different job and a different part of the same organisation were more likely to be working longer hours. So too were those working at senior management levels.

Given these long hours, do workers believe they have the right balance between home and work? 78 per cent believe that they have. This compares with 75 per cent who said they had the right balance in 1998. Not surprisingly, it is those

working longer hours in senior management positions who are most likely to say they have the wrong balance. Interestingly, those on temporary contracts are among those most likely to report that they have the right balance between work and life outside work. Among those who think they have the wrong balance, almost everyone – 94 per cent – said that work dominates. This confirms what our previous studies and many other studies have shown, namely that for some people work, and in particular long working hours, has become a tyranny or perhaps an addiction. But it is a tyranny or addiction less for the traditional working classes than for the senior managers and professionals, the well-educated and the well-paid.

General life satisfaction

Although it is not necessarily central to behaviour at work, we collected information about wider satisfaction with life as a whole on the assumption that this may be linked to experience at work. This is again a repeat of questions asked in previous years and the results are shown in Table 9.

Table 9 | Satisfaction with aspects of life

% (n = 493)	Satisfaction levels						
	Low 1–3		Medium 4–7		High 8–10		Average
	1998	1999	1998	1999	1998	1999	1999
SATISFACTION WITH							
Your life as a whole	3	3	40	38	57	59	7.52
Your family	3	3	20	15	77	82	8.55
Your friends	1	1	27	27	71	72	8.12
Your health	3	3	29	27	68	69	7.90
Your work	5	8	46	49	49	43	6.87
Your finances	10	10	49	52	41	37	6.51

Notes

1 Numbers are rounded and will therefore not always sum to 100 per cent.

2 Items are rated on a 10-point scale, where 1=totally dissatisfied and 10=totally satisfied.

The pattern of results is very similar to previous years, with family and friends a major source of satisfaction and work and finances evaluated much more cautiously. Only 3 per cent in this sample rate their satisfaction with life as a whole as low. It is possible to treat these six items as a single general indicator of life satisfaction. In 1998 those most likely to report high satisfaction with life as a whole were more likely to have a positive psychological contract, to have the right balance between home and work, to be married as opposed to single or divorced, to be female, to work longer hours, to be in service jobs and to be quite strongly committed to home life.

Although job change may have affected life satisfaction, for consistency we examine changes only for the 493 who are in the same job with the same employer at the time of the 1999 survey. The first thing to note is that responses to these items on life satisfaction are highly stable, so there is only a limited amount of change to examine. Bearing this in mind – and acknowledging that

factors outside the workplace that we have not measured may have an important influence – among the items that were measured, an improvement in life satisfaction over the year was found among those who had a positive psychological contract, who reported higher levels of direct participation and among blue-collar workers. The results are summarised in Figure 5.

Summary of attitude items

We have now reviewed the full set of attitude items within the conceptual framework of the psychological contract. They confirm that the state of the psychological contract is a strong explanatory factor, both at a specific point in time and as a predictor over time. The results presented so far also show a small but consistent decline in attitudes between 1998 and 1999. Most of the changes are not statistically significant, confirming the relative stability of these measures. The notable exception is the measure of the state of the psychological contract, but this can be largely

Figure 5 | Changes in life satisfaction

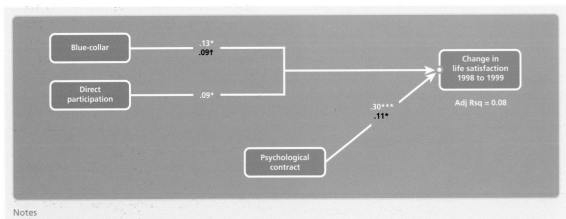

Notes

1   † slightly significant (p<.10); * significant (p<.05); ** strongly significant (p<.01); *** very strongly significant (p<.001). Only significant associations are displayed.

2   Black numbers present 1998 associations; white numbers present 1999 associations.

' ... there is evidence of a significant decline in the reported use of the type of progressive human resource practices that have a positive influence on the state of the psychological contract ... .'

explained by the use of a slightly different question. Our previous surveys, which did not have the advantage of longitudinal analysis, suggested that attitudes were more or less stable between 1997 and 1998 after improving between 1996 and 1997. At the same time, there is evidence of a significant decline in the reported use of the type of progressive human resource practices that have a positive influence on the state of the psychological contract and, in turn, on attitudes. There is also a decline in the scope for direct participation. This does not bode well for future attitudes. By implication, the problem and the remedy lie in the hands of management.

Behaviour at work

While workers might be primarily concerned with their experience of and attitudes towards work

and its impact on their well-being and their life as a whole, for employers a more important concern is work behaviour and its determinants. Several aspects of behaviour at work are explored each year in the survey. A number have been examined in more depth in previous surveys and this year we use only one or two items, taken from a larger set, to explore each aspect of behaviour. However, we shall, as in previous years, examine the influence of a range of background factors and attitudes on employee behaviour to determine the policy implications. The analysis is more powerful because we can explore the impact of practices and attitudes in 1998 on behaviour in 1999.

Motivation

Two items were used to explore motivation in both surveys. These tap a general aspect of what can probably be characterised as intrinsic motivation. The results for the two years are shown in Table 10.

Table 10 | Motivation

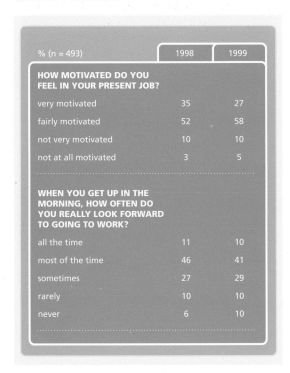

% (n = 493)	1998	1999
HOW MOTIVATED DO YOU FEEL IN YOUR PRESENT JOB?		
very motivated	35	27
fairly motivated	52	58
not very motivated	10	10
not at all motivated	3	5
WHEN YOU GET UP IN THE MORNING, HOW OFTEN DO YOU REALLY LOOK FORWARD TO GOING TO WORK?		
all the time	11	10
most of the time	46	41
sometimes	27	29
rarely	10	10
never	6	10

The results in Table 10 indicate a small but significant reduction in reported levels of motivation. We need to explore the background factors that might help to explain this. First we should note, based on the results in 1998, that higher levels of motivation are associated with higher commitment to the organisation, life satisfaction, emotional involvement in work, positive assessment of employer–employee relations, a positive psychological contract, higher levels of direct participation and being older. When we look at what predicts changes in the motivation, we find that age, level of education and sense of job security have a marginally significant influence. When we incorporate current attitudes, then a range of attitudinal influences have a positive effect. These include current job satisfaction, organisational commitment and the state of the psychological contract. Level of education is also significant, while age remains marginally significant. By implication, a reduction in any of these would help to explain the small drop in motivation between 1998 and 1999. The results for motivation and the next variable, effort, are summarised in Figure 6.

Figure 6 | Changes in motivation and effort

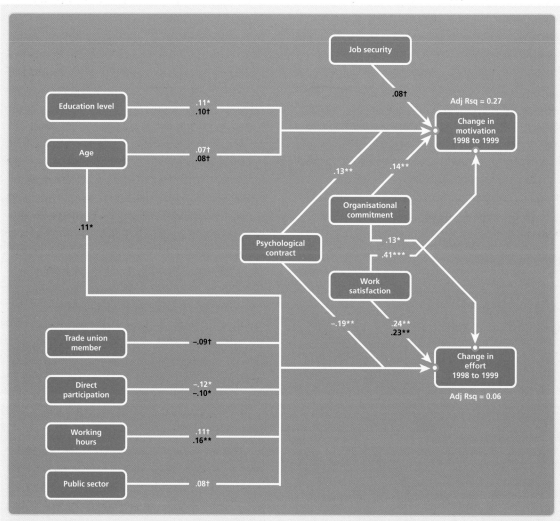

Notes

1 † slightly significant (p<.10); * significant (p<.05); ** strongly significant (p<.01); *** very strongly significant (p<.001). Only significant associations are displayed.

2 Black numbers present 1998 associations; white numbers present 1999 associations.

Effort

In theory, effort is closely related to motivation. However, our previous surveys have shown consistently that it covers a different dimension. Indeed, it is more concerned with externally imposed demands rather than those freely chosen by workers. It therefore has elements of obligation and imposition within it and fewer of the positive connotations associated with intrinsic motivation. The items covering effort are shown in Table 11.

Comparison of the 1998 and 1999 results among those in the same jobs shows no significant changes in levels of effort over the year. In the 1998 survey, effort was reported as higher among women, those highly committed to the organisation, those who work in the private rather than the public sector, those who have a lower income, a poorer psychological contract, the wrong balance between home and work and a high level of emotional involvement in work. The only aspects in common with motivation are high levels of commitment and emotional involvement in work. Notably, effort is associated with a poorer psychological contract.

If we look at what predicts *changes* in the level of effort, we find a range of positive and negative influences. Job satisfaction and working hours in 1998 and age predict an increase in effort between 1998 and 1999. Direct participation predicts a decrease in effort; so too, marginally, does trade union membership. If we look at 1999 attitudes, then increased effort is still strongly associated with job satisfaction and now also with commitment, and marginally associated with working hours and working in the public sector. Reduced levels of effort are associated with direct participation and a more positive psychological contract. These results seem to confirm that workers who are satisfied and committed are likely to put in more effort. Their commitment and effort are already manifested in working longer hours. However, those with more control through direct participation will not choose to increase their effort, nor will those who already believe that they have a poorer psychological contract, perhaps because of the excessive demands of the job or the inequity of the effort–reward bargain. These results, which are summarised in Figure 6, appear to confirm the important influence of workers' attitudes on the level of effort they put into their work.

Table 11 | Effort

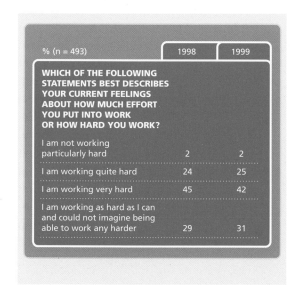

% (n = 493)	1998	1999
WHICH OF THE FOLLOWING STATEMENTS BEST DESCRIBES YOUR CURRENT FEELINGS ABOUT HOW MUCH EFFORT YOU PUT INTO WORK OR HOW HARD YOU WORK?		
I am not working particularly hard	2	2
I am working quite hard	24	25
I am working very hard	45	42
I am working as hard as I can and could not imagine being able to work any harder	29	31

Innovative behaviour

Three items explored aspects of innovation. The wording and response categories are slightly adapted from those used in previous years, so direct comparisons are a little risky. The responses for 1998 and 1999 are shown in Table 12.

The results in Table 12 show that on each item, somewhere between one-quarter and one-third often suggest innovations in work while at the other extreme about one-fifth say they do this rarely or never. When we look at the 1998 results, innovation is associated with being more senior, with direct participation, more human resource practices, higher organisational commitment and a higher level of general satisfaction with life but also with a poorer psychological contract.

Bearing in mind the small changes in the way in which the questions were asked, we can still tentatively explore changes in response between 1998 and 1999. However, we must exercise even more caution than usual in reading too much into the results, which appear to show a statistically significant increase in levels of innovative

behaviour. The analysis shows that those working longer hours in 1998 were likely to report a marginally significant increase in levels of innovative behaviour while those on temporary contracts were likely to report a significant decrease. Incorporating 1999 attitudes, we find that an increase in innovation is significantly associated with more scope for direct participation, higher levels of commitment and more human resource practices and it remains significantly reduced among those on temporary contracts. These results fit with other research suggesting that job design, reflected in scope for direct participation, is a key influence on innovative behaviour. The negative influence of being on a temporary contract is not unexpected; it should be noted that it does not extend to those on fixed-term contracts. The results for innovation and for the next variable, organisational citizenship, are shown in Figure 7.

Organisational citizenship behaviour

Organisational citizenship is concerned with the extent to which people are willing to go beyond their formal role to do things for the organisation.

Table 12 | Innovative behaviour

% (n = 493)	Often		Sometimes		Rarely		Never	
	1998	1999	1998	1999	1998	1999	1998	1999
In the past year, how often have you:								
thought of ideas for improving the organisation and shared these with your co-workers?	20	34	54	49	14	6	12	11
made innovative suggestions to help improve your department?	24	29	57	56	10	7	9	8
thought of ideas for improving co-worker performance and shared these with co-workers?	23	24	53	50	14	12	10	13

Note: Numbers are rounded and will therefore not always sum to 100 per cent.

Figure 7 | Changes in citizenship behaviours and innovative behaviour

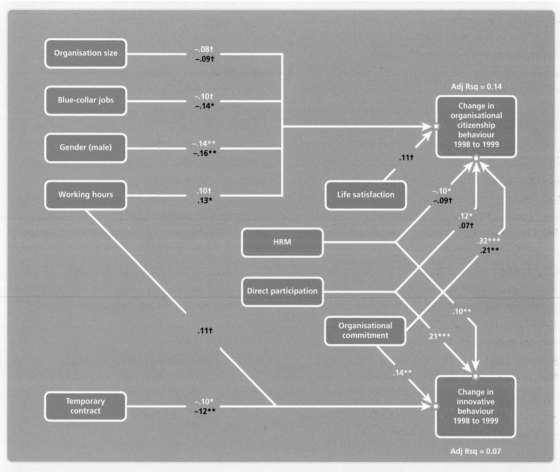

Notes

1 † slightly significant (p<.10); * significant (p<.05); ** strongly significant (p<.01); *** very strongly significant (p<.001). Only significant associations are displayed.

2 Black numbers present 1998 associations; white numbers present 1999 associations.

> 'Increased citizenship behaviour is now found among those
> with high commitment to the organisation and also those with
> high levels of direct participation ... .'

It should be noted that the question is concerned with obligation rather than pure desire to be helpful, so it may not tap a totally voluntary kind of behaviour. The results in 1999 and the 1998 comparisons for the 493 in the same jobs are shown in Table 13.

The results in Table 13 suggest that most people do feel some obligation to engage in citizenship behaviour. We can get some indication of whether this is born of a sense of commitment or duty and whether or not it is resented by exploring background factors and attitudes associated with varying levels of citizenship behaviour. In 1998, those reporting higher levels of organisational citizenship behaviour were more likely to have higher levels of organisational commitment, to be female, to report the wrong balance between home and work as well as that home was less of a central interest in their lives, to be managers and professionals rather than blue-collar workers and to feel less secure in their jobs. These results confirm an element of obligation and possibly of dissatisfaction and anxiety. But these are combined

with a high level of commitment to the organisation, which helps to explain why workers engage in this type of behaviour.

A comparison among those in the same jobs indicates a significant decrease over the year in reported levels of citizenship behaviour. If we look at what predicts *changes* in citizenship behaviour between 1998 and 1999, we find that it has increased significantly among those who reported high commitment in 1998 and among those working longer hours. It has decreased significantly among blue-collar workers and men, and marginally significantly among those reporting higher levels of general satisfaction with life, among those reporting more human resource practices and those working in larger organisations. When we incorporate current attitudes, the results alter only a little. Increased citizenship behaviour is now found among those with high commitment to the organisation and also those with high levels of direct participation while working hours remain marginally significant. Decreased citizenship is still significantly associated

Table 13 | Organisational citizenship behaviour

| % (n = 493) | no obligation at all | | | | | | very strong obligation | | | |
| | 1 | | 2 | | 3 | | 4 | | 5 | |
	1998	1999	1998	1999	1998	1999	1998	1999	1998	1999
To what extent do you feel obliged to:										
go to work even if you do not feel particularly well	13	11	7	10	21	22	24	25	35	32
show loyalty to the organisation	4	5	4	6	20	25	29	29	43	36
work overtime or extra hours when required	9	12	8	9	21	24	26	22	36	32
volunteer to do tasks outside your job description	18	14	11	15	26	31	27	26	18	14

Note: Numbers are rounded and will therefore not always sum to 100 per cent.

with male workers and with more human resource practices. There is a marginally significant association with blue-collar workers and with larger organisations. These results are summarised in Figure 7. Perhaps the most puzzling finding is that those who experience more human resource practices report a decrease in citizenship behaviour. One explanation might be that these practices reduce the need for such behaviour: organisational systems and practices take over some of the support activities. Another might be that where human resource practices include job design and team-working, citizenship behaviour, which is sometimes described as extra-role behaviour, is more likely to be incorporated into the job.

Work performance

In previous surveys it has proved difficult to obtain useful ratings of performance at work within a survey of this sort. This year we therefore retained a single item that seeks to capture change in performance. This is shown in Table 14.

Table 14 | Change in work performance

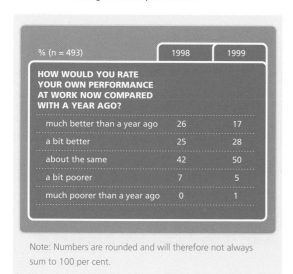

% (n = 493)	1998	1999
HOW WOULD YOU RATE YOUR OWN PERFORMANCE AT WORK NOW COMPARED WITH A YEAR AGO?		
much better than a year ago	26	17
a bit better	25	28
about the same	42	50
a bit poorer	7	5
much poorer than a year ago	0	1

Note: Numbers are rounded and will therefore not always sum to 100 per cent.

The results in Table 14 show a trend towards saying that performance had stayed the same rather than improving over the year. In 1998, those who felt that their performance had improved over the year tended to have a shorter tenure, to be younger, to be on lower incomes, to report more human resource practices in place, to have lower levels of education, to work in larger organisations and to have a lower than average level of job security. There is a plausible suggestion in these results that performance improvement is greatest among those who are less experienced and therefore have most scope to improve. What predicts performance improvement in 1999? Only three factors emerge. Performance improvement is significantly greater among those who are younger, who work in the service sector and who report that more human resource practices are in place.

When we turn to contemporary influences on self-rated performance improvement, several additional factors become important. Being younger, working in the service sector and reporting more human resource practices all remain significant. In addition, performance improvement is associated with higher commitment and satisfaction and with greater scope for direct participation. Although it is only marginal, those on fixed-term contracts are more likely to report reduced performance. The full results are set out in Figure 8. These findings are interesting in supporting the wider literature on a link between progressive human resource practices and performance improvement. While we must be cautious about self-report measures of performance, the fact that this finding appears in the longitudinal analysis as well as in the cross-sectional analysis suggests that it is a relatively robust causal link.

Intention to quit

Four items looked at the intention to quit. These are shown in Table 15.

There is only one item in this section on which comparison over the two years is possible. This shows a significant increase in the proportion who say they are looking around for other jobs or currently in the process of trying to leave. The figures show a high level of potential movement with over half sometimes or frequently looking at job advertisements and over 40 per cent saying that sometimes or often they have seriously considered leaving. Over one-third have looked around for other jobs or are currently in the process of trying to move. However, the proportion who believe it is very likely that they

Figure 8 | Change in work performance and the intention to quit

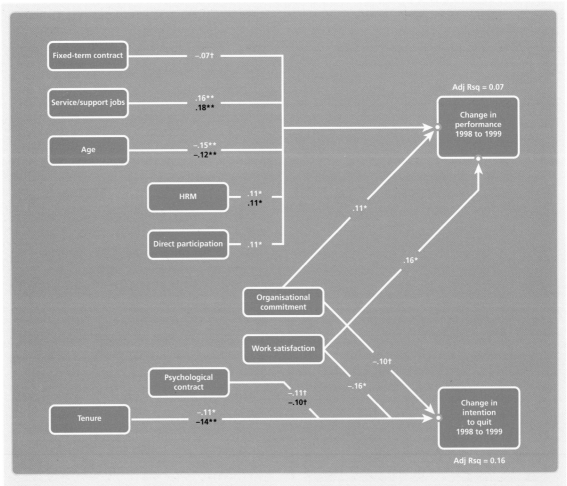

Notes

1 † slightly significant (p<.10); * significant (p<.05); ** strongly significant (p<.01); *** very strongly significant (p<.001). Only significant associations are displayed.

2 Black numbers present 1998 associations; white numbers present 1999 associations.

will leave their current job in the next year is much lower at just 12 per cent. Nevertheless, we know that intention to leave is the best predictor of whether people actually leave their jobs and these results reveal quite a high propensity to move on. This raises important questions about who the likely leavers are. Those saying they are very likely to leave their jobs in the next year are either those in temporary jobs or those who have changed organisation in the past year; the two categories may overlap. By way of slight contrast, those who are most likely to say they are currently in the process of trying to change jobs are those on fixed-term contracts. In other words, those who are most likely to be mobile in the future are those who already have recent experience of labour market mobility.

If we look at the results for 1998, these reveal that attitudinal factors were most closely associated with intention to quit. Those most likely to say they might move reported a poorer psychological contract, poorer employment relations, lower commitment, higher emotional involvement in work, lower general life satisfaction and the wrong balance between home and work. They also had a higher level of education and higher scope for direct participation. This implies that labour turnover is likely to be highest among relatively well-educated and marketable people

Table 15 | Intention to quit

% (n = 493)	Often	Sometimes	Rarely	Never
How often during the past year have you:				
seriously considered leaving the organisation?	16	27	21	36
looked for job advertisements in newspapers to which you could apply?	21	27	22	30

	1998	1999
WHICH OF THE FOLLOWING STATEMENTS BEST DESCRIBES YOU?		
I have never even thought about leaving this job	40	24
I have sometimes thought about leaving this job	35	42
I have looked around for other jobs	18	24
I am currently in the process of trying to leave this job	8	10
HOW LIKELY IS IT THAT YOU WILL QUIT THIS JOB IN THE FOLLOWING YEAR?		
not at all likely	–	58
slightly likely	–	22
fairly likely	–	8
very likely	–	12

Note: Numbers are rounded and will therefore not always sum to 100 per cent.

> ' ... the results reinforce the importance of a link from the use of progressive human resource practices and a climate of direct participation to a positive psychological contract and through this to attitudes and in turn behaviour.'

who are seeking involvement in work but not getting it in their present job.

What factors are associated with *change* in the intention to quit? Here the results are less helpful. Nothing measured in 1998 predicts an increased propensity to quit by 1999. But longer tenure and to a lesser extent a positive psychological contract are likely to reduce the intention to leave. When we look at current attitudes, the results are even less clear-cut. Only tenure is significantly associated with a lower propensity to quit. Higher levels of commitment and work satisfaction also have a marginally significant influence. This suggests that increased likelihood of leaving will be associated with the opposite of the factors identified – low commitment, satisfaction and tenure – or with factors in the labour market that lie outside the scope of this survey. The results are summarised in Figure 8.

Summary

The survey has explored changes in behaviour over a year and the influences on them. The general trend is to slightly reduce the level of contribution. This is reflected in lower motivation, less citizenship behaviour and an increased propensity to look for jobs elsewhere. The main factors explaining these changes seem to be workers' attitudes. Going one step further, the results reinforce the importance of a link from the use of progressive human resource practices and a climate of direct participation to a positive psychological contract and through this to attitudes and in turn behaviour. Workers report that organisations are showing a reduced concern for human resource practices and for direct participation and this is beginning to feed through into less positive attitudes and work-related behaviour. The 1999 analysis provides a clear warning to management.

3 | Change in employment status

◻ **Those most likely to have left employment between 1998 and 1999 were already on the margins of employment.**

◻ **A change of job seems to be good for most people. Those who changed jobs report higher levels of satisfaction, commitment and motivation than a year ago.**

◻ **After a job change, those who stood out in 1998 for their generally negative attitudes were similar in attitude and behaviour to the majority of workers.**

Each year, millions of people change jobs. Most do so voluntarily. Yet in some cases, change in employment can be a painful experience for the individual and a significant loss to the employer. In the tight labour market that operates at present, it is often in the interests of organisations to retain as many employees as possible and in particular to hold on to key employees.

In our sample of 619, all of whom had been in employment when they were first interviewed in 1998, 15.7 per cent had changed their employment in some way. This is probably an underestimate of the actual amount of movement in the labour market since a number of those we were unable to contact to re-interview will have moved home, possibly in the context of a change in employment. When they were interviewed in 1999, 37 (6.0 per cent) were not in employment and a further 60 (9.7 per cent) had changed their employer. A further 29 (4.7 per cent) had moved to another job within the same organisation. In addition, a number in the sample had changed their employment contracts. It is these groups that form the focus of this chapter.

Those not in employment

Of the 37 who were not in employment, 27 chose to leave and 10 were forced to leave. Among those forced to leave, half were made redundant, two left because of illness, one was dismissed and one came to the end of a contract. Among the 27 who chose to leave, 14 left for personal reasons, including pregnancy/childbirth (6), retirement (5) and personal or family illness (3). Nine left to get away from what they were doing, claiming they were fed up with work (3), had no prospects (3), were bored with the job (2) or faced problems with their boss (1). The remaining four cited inconvenient hours, end of contract, the desire to become self-employed and no reason. The point about labouring these reasons is to show that no more than one-third of those who are no longer in employment left directly as a response to poor management policy and practice. Most left their jobs either at the initiative of management, as in the case of redundancies, or due to personal factors beyond the control of management.

> ' … most people left because what they were doing was no longer attractive; by implication, some of this is under management control.'

Despite the apparent inevitability of many of the reasons for not being in employment, and bearing in mind the need for caution because the numbers involved are small, we can see some factors in 1998 that help to differentiate those not in work in 1999. For example, based on a simple correlational analysis, in 1998 they were more likely to be on a temporary (but not a fixed-term) rather than a permanent contract. They were less likely to be a trade union member. Also, they were more likely to work fewer hours and to have a lower income. Finally, they were less likely to say they took part in any organisational citizenship behaviours, which might possibly be an initial sign of 'withdrawal' behaviour. In other words, those who moved out of employment were more likely to be those already on the margins of employment. Employers are unlikely to be dismayed to see them go. Indeed, only 14 of the 37 are actively looking for work.

Those who change job

Sixty people in the sample changed their employer over the year. Analysis of the reasons reveals that the majority left for negative or 'push' reasons – in other words, to get away from what they were doing. Of the 60, 19 (32 per cent) cited poor pay and prospects; 11 (18 per cent) said the job was boring or too easy while only one said it was too demanding; 8 (13 per cent) saw no scope for development; and four just wanted a break or were fed up with work. A further 23 per cent said that either the hours or the location were inconvenient; 13 per cent said that they had no choice but to move because of the end of a contract, redundancy or company closure. Finally, 10 (17 per cent) cited positive or 'pull' factors, such as being offered a better job, career advancement or career change. It can be seen

from this that some people gave more than one reason for moving. The key point to note is that most people left because what they were doing was no longer attractive; by implication, some of this is under management control.

Given this, can we see in advance who is more or less likely to change jobs? If we look at the 1998 results and correlate them with job change, then a predictable pattern emerges. In terms of individual characteristics, the job changers are younger, have a shorter tenure, are less likely to be breadwinners and are more likely to be single. Turning to organisational features, they are likely to have experienced fewer progressive human resource practices, they are less likely to belong to a trade union and they report a poorer psychological contract. In terms of attitudes and behaviour, in 1998 they reported lower commitment, lower satisfaction, poorer employment relations, poorer life satisfaction, lower job security, lower motivation and, perhaps predictably, a higher intention to quit. In other words, there were some strong indicators in the previous year about who was likely to change jobs. Furthermore, 73 per cent of those who have changed organisation felt that it was their own choice compared with 18 per cent who felt it was forced upon them by circumstances; in other words, they felt they were in control of the situation.

We undertook an analysis that explored the impact of change in employer on changes in attitudes and behaviour between the 1998 and 1999 surveys. This is a strict test, since it controls for all other possible influences. This reveals that a change of employer is associated with an improved psychological contract, increased work satisfaction and a lower level of engagement in organisational citizenship behaviours. This last finding can probably be explained by inevitably being new to the organisation and therefore not yet in a position to get fully involved in citizenship-type activities.

The interesting question arises as to whether these job changers are generally less satisfied and more mobile or whether their reactions are context specific. This can be gauged from the 1999 survey. In terms of whether or not they are generally better off, the results are overwhelming – 83 per cent said the change is something they wanted and only 15 per cent preferred where they were a year ago. They are now just as satisfied and committed as the typical worker in the sample. They are more likely to report that their job performance has improved. In short, both they and the organisation to which they have moved, appear to have benefited from the change. Even allowing for a certain amount of post hoc justification on the part of those who have moved, this suggests that the consequences of job change have been positive for most of the workers in this group.

Change in contract of employment

Although it is less central to the analysis, we did explore the amount of movement between types of employment contract. Of the 45 who were on temporary contracts in 1998, only 30 per cent were still in temporary employment in 1999; 33 per cent had obtained permanent jobs, 18 per cent now had fixed-term contracts and 20 per cent were not in employment. This confirms the transitory nature of temporary contracts. In contrast, among the 40 on fixed-term contracts, 37 per cent remained on a fixed-term contract, 45 per cent now had permanent jobs, 10 per cent had moved on to temporary contracts and 7 per

cent were not in employment. Finally, among those in permanent jobs in 1998, 7 per cent had moved on to fixed-term contracts, 5 per cent on to temporary contracts and 6 per cent were not in work. Numbers in the sample are too small to justify a detailed analysis of the causes and consequences of contract change.

Who chooses to leave?

We have already shown that it is possible to predict who will be more likely to change jobs between 1998 and 1999 by examining background, work experiences and attitudes in 1998. We can take this one step further by identifying those who are likely to leave voluntarily, whether to start a new job or to become unemployed. This is a slightly different analysis since it includes only those who choose to act in this way and we might expect that attitudes and work experiences will be more important. The initial step in the analysis was to look for any significant correlation between 1998 responses and subsequently choosing to leave. This shows that those most likely to leave of their own accord are, in order of the size of the correlation:

- more likely to have stated their intention to leave
- less likely to be a trade union member
- more likely to be on a lower income and in a temporary contract
- less likely to say they engage in organisational citizenship behaviours
- younger

> ' ... those who are not currently in employment left their jobs mainly
> for personal reasons, often linked to personal or family health, or
> through a management-initiated redundancy programme.'

◰ shorter service

◰ female

◰ less likely to work long hours

◰ less committed

◰ less motivated.

These findings are largely endorsed in a more rigorous discriminant analysis in which intention to leave again emerges as the key predictor. In summary, there is already a pattern of low commitment and contribution in 1998 and stated intention to quit remains a strong predictor of actual voluntary labour turnover.

Summary

This chapter has focused on change in employment reflected either in moving out of employment, changing employer or changing employment contract status. It reveals that those who are not currently in employment left their jobs mainly for personal reasons, often linked to personal or family health, or through a management-initiated redundancy programme. Few just quit and not surprisingly, therefore, only a minority are actively seeking work. Most who change employer cite 'push' factors encouraging them to leave their previous employer. In 1998 this was a much more dissatisfied group, but by 1999, after the job change, they were just as satisfied as the working population as a whole. It is worth noting that their age and commitments meant that they were also a more mobile group. For them, the change has been positive. There may be lessons for the organisations that have lost them since, in 1998, these workers reported below average use of human resource practices by their employer and a poorer psychological contract with their employer. Finally, analysis of employment contracts confirms that those on temporary contracts are closer to the margins of employment and more likely to have stopped working during the year. In contrast, those on fixed-term contracts were no more likely to have stopped working than those on permanent contracts.

4 | The experience of organisational change

◘ **The strong negative impact of redundancy programmes on workers who stay suggests that organisations are still paying disproportionate attention to those who leave at the expense of workers who stay.**

◘ **Most changes reported suggest that jobs are becoming more demanding and more challenging. But asked whether this makes the job better or worse, a majority said it made no real difference.**

◘ **Changes in personnel policies are generally viewed more negatively than many other kinds of change.**

◘ **Workers recognise that they have to learn to live with change and most now accept it as a part of everyday organisational life.**

This chapter focuses on change within organisations. There has been much discussion about the experience of change and its generally negative consequences for workers. The view is often expressed that there is too much change going on. This chapter seeks to put this assumption to the test by gauging how much change is reported, what type of change, how workers react to change and what consequences it has for attitudes and behaviour. This is where the analysis over the two years becomes particularly useful, since we can compare how change during the intervening period has affected a number of outcomes such as satisfaction, motivation and intention to quit. If change is negative, we should expect attitudes to have deteriorated. Furthermore, because we can control for other factors, we can be reasonably confident that any shift in attitudes and behaviour is a consequence of the changes.

Change within organisations can occur at a number of levels. In the following sections we explore change at the levels of the organisation, the workplace and then the job. In some cases, change will have been experienced at all levels. We then explore general attitudes towards change at work.

Organisational change

49 per cent said their organisation had been going through some kind of change programme during the past year. We asked about six specific types of organisational change. Among those reporting changes:

◘ 65 per cent said there had been restructuring

◘ 47 per cent cited new technology

◘ 36 per cent mentioned general reorganisation of their work

◘ 35 per cent cited redundancies or staff reductions

◘ 34 per cent cited a merger or acquisition

◘ 22 per cent cited culture change.

A number of people cited more than one of these types of change and a further 8 per cent said other types of organisational change had occurred. Perhaps the main surprise in these responses is the high proportion saying that there had been a merger or acquisition.

' ... change was significantly more likely to be reported by those working in larger organisations and larger establishments ... .'

What sort of people, and in what sort of context, were more likely to predict experience of organisational change? The first thing we looked at was whether any organisational change had been experienced and we conducted a discriminant analysis to identify organisational and individual factors that distinguished those who said they had and had not experienced organisational change. This revealed that change was significantly more likely to be reported by those working in larger organisations and larger establishments, by men, by those in manufacturing rather than service industry, but not by those on temporary contracts. The second step was to explore the amount of change. As noted above, we asked about six types of organisational change. We therefore compared those who reported a high level of change, represented by change in

four or more of the six items (12 per cent of workers) against those who reported less change (31 per cent) or no change (57 per cent). This produced a similar pattern of results. More change had occurred among those working in larger organisations and larger establishments, among men, among those with higher incomes and among those working longer hours. Public sector workers reported significantly less change.

Whether change is seen as positive or negative is likely to depend partly on the type of change. We explored the background factors that explained experience of particular types of organisational change. The results are summarised in Table 16. The table shows the factors that discriminate between those who had and had not experienced each type of change. Several other background

Table 16 | Background factors predicting experience of organisational change

% (n = 493)	Redundancy	Restructuring	Merger	New Technology	Reorganisation of your work	Culture Change
Organisation size	+**	+***	+**	+**		+**
Establishment size	+**	+**	+**	+*		+*
Manufacturing sector	+***					
Public sector				–*		
Service jobs	–**					
Male	+*	+*	+**	+*		+*
Income			+*			+***
Hours			+**			+**
Education level						+**
Management level						+***

A plus sign indicates that the type of change, shown in the top row, is significantly likely to be associated with the background variables shown in the left-hand column. For example, redundancy is more likely to occur in larger organisations, larger establishments in the manufacturing sector and to men but less likely among those in service and support jobs. The minus sign indicates a negative association. As in most other tables, the asterisks show the level of statistical significance of the association (* significant, p<.05; ** strongly significant, p<.01; *** very strongly significant, p<.001). Where there is a blank, there is no significant association.

items were included but did not show any significant discrimination.

The results in Table 16 confirm the pattern for change in general. Greater change is likely to have occurred in larger organisations and establishments and to be experienced by men. It is notable that none of the background organisational or individual factors predicts reorganisation of work and that culture change is more likely to be reported by those in senior positions as reflected by education, management level and income. This may reflect a view of what constitutes culture change. Some changes defined as culture change by senior staff may be perceived as something else by more junior staff.

How does organisational change affect the psychological contract and general attitudes and behaviour at work? Some of the American literature on the psychological contract sees change as a potential violation of the psychological contract. While it is conceivable that this may be the case for certain types of change, can we generalise to all changes at work? We can start by exploring whether it is the amount of change that matters. To determine this, we compared those who had experienced varying amounts of organisational change. The results are summarised in Table 17.

The results in Table 17 show that the amount of change has a moderate and predominantly

Table 17 | Impact of amount of organisational change on attitudes and behaviour

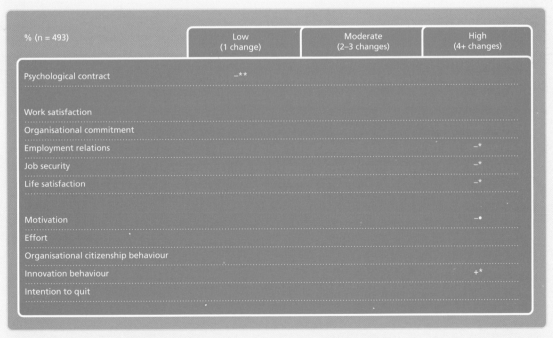

% (n = 493)	Low (1 change)	Moderate (2–3 changes)	High (4+ changes)
Psychological contract	–**		
Work satisfaction			
Organisational commitment			
Employment relations			–*
Job security			–*
Life satisfaction			–*
Motivation			–•
Effort			
Organisational citizenship behaviour			
Innovation behaviour			+*
Intention to quit			

The plus or minus signs indicate whether the change was viewed as positive or negative. Asterisks indicate the level of statistical significance with * significant (p<.05) and ** strongly significant (p<.01). The referent category in the analysis, against which the others are compared, is no change.

> '**Redundancy programmes have a clear and consistently
> negative impact on attitudes and, to a much lesser
> extent, behaviour.**'

negative impact. More specifically, larger amounts of change have a negative impact on employment relations, job security, life satisfaction and motivation, but a positive impact on innovative behaviour. A more unexpected result is the negative impact on the psychological contract of a small amount of change. Although the size effects are generally small, there is some evidence to support the view that large amounts of organisational change have a negative effect on attitudes. We cannot generalise this to behaviour, implying that it is workers rather than organisations that suffer the effects of large-scale organisational change.

The second thing we can look at is the specific type of change. We can examine the impact of each type of organisational change on the

attitudes and behaviour of workers. The significant results are shown in Table 18. This shows the results for the four types of organisational change that had a significant impact. The two that are omitted – mergers and acquisitions and culture change – had no significant impact on any attitudes or behaviour.

The results in Table 18 confirm the importance of looking at the type of organisational change before reaching conclusions about organisational change in general. First, we should note that four of the six types of organisational change had little or no impact on attitudes and behaviour. These include mergers and acquisitions, culture change, restructuring and work reorganisation. These are important results for a number of reasons. First, it is surprising that mergers and acquisitions have

Table 18 | Impact of specific changes on attitudes and behaviour

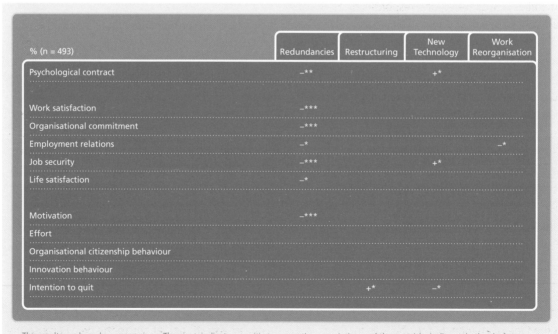

% (n = 493)	Redundancies	Restructuring	New Technology	Work Reorganisation
Psychological contract	–**		+*	
Work satisfaction	–***			
Organisational commitment	–***			
Employment relations	–*			–*
Job security	–***		+*	
Life satisfaction	–*			
Motivation	–***			
Effort				
Organisational citizenship behaviour				
Innovation behaviour				
Intention to quit		+*	–*	

The results are based on regressions. The signs indicate a positive or negative association and the asterisks indicate the level of statistical significance association (* significant, p<.05; ** strongly significant, p<.01; *** very strongly significant, p<.001).

little or no impact. One explanation may be that these have more impact at the top of the organisation, at least in the short term, than lower down. Only when they begin to have an impact through redundancies are larger numbers of workers directly affected. Second, work restructuring, reorganisation and more particularly culture change programmes have little or no effect despite their deliberate attempt to influence attitudes and behaviour. This supports other evidence suggesting that many culture change programmes are likely to fail to achieve their goals. Where restructuring and reorganisation have an impact, it is negative, harming industrial relations and increasing the propensity to quit.

The two types of organisational change that have a more marked impact have directly opposite effects. Redundancy programmes have a clear and consistently negative impact on attitudes and, to a much lesser extent, behaviour. It is important to remember that these are the responses of the 'survivors' rather than those who have been made redundant. This suggests that there is something about the way in which redundancies are handled, whether they are voluntary or compulsory redundancies, that sends negative signals to those who stay. It is also an endorsement of those organisations that promote explicit policies of avoiding redundancies if at all possible. In contrast, the introduction of new technology is consistently associated with increasingly positive attitudes among workers. It improves the psychological contract, enhances job security and reduces the desire to leave the organisation.

In summary, large-scale organisational change tends to have a negative impact on attitudes though not on behaviour. However, much depends on the type of change. Some changes that are designed to have an impact on attitudes and

behaviour fail to do so while others have either a consistently positive or negative impact. It appears that management still has much to learn about managing the process of organisational change to the benefit of both workers and the organisation.

Workplace change

A second level at which changes can occur is more locally in the workplace. Changes at this level may be affected by larger-scale organisational change or they can take place in their own right. A set of fairly specific questions about change at workplace level were asked of the 493 workers who were doing the same job as a year ago. A factor analysis showed that these changes clustered into three groups according to whether the change was concerned with aspects of job and work design, new technology and products, or working arrangements linked to terms and conditions of employment. The results are shown in Table 19.

Perhaps the interesting general point to note about the results in Table 19 is that on all but two of the items a majority say things are the same as a year ago. This fits with the responses on organisational change. The second point is that across all the items there are none where as many as 10 per cent report a decline or reduction. The two items on which a majority report change are the introduction of new technology and how hard you work. Previous surveys have revealed that a majority of workers believe that they are working ever harder. The reports about redundancies and workforce reductions provide some basis for this claim.

We examined the factors that predicted workplace change. In doing so, we omitted the third factor concerned with alterations to the deal because the two items did not combine into an acceptable

> **' ... both the number of human resource practices and the scope for direct participation are strongly associated with a better psychological contract.'**

scale. We first explored general background factors. Changes in job and work design were more likely to be reported by those on fixed-term contracts, an issue we return to in a later section, and less likely to be reported by older workers and by trade union members. Changes in new technology and products were more likely to be reported by those with longer tenure. In each case, these groups are likely to say that there has been an increase rather than a decrease.

One issue of particular interest is any link to larger-scale organisational change. This reveals that with respect to job design, at the organisational level redundancies have a negative impact on job design issues, while mergers, workplace reorganisation and culture change all have a significant positive effect. Turning to new technology and products, redundancies again have a negative impact while organisational-level change in technology, not surprisingly, has a positive impact. While there is some overlap between levels, especially in smaller organisations, this brief analysis confirms that organisation-level changes filter through to workplace-level changes. Redundancies appear to inhibit workplace change

Table 19 | Experience of workplace change

% (n = 493)	Gone up a lot	Gone up a little	Stayed the same	Gone down a little	Gone down a lot
JOB AND WORK DESIGN					
How hard you work	18	31	46	5	1
The amount of influence over the way you do your work	13	27	56	4	0
Challenge and excitement in your job	7	24	61	5	3
Your opportunity to work closely with others in a team	8	18	72	2	1
Your opportunity to work closer to your customers	5	9	83	1	1
Responsibilities you have in your job	16	30	54	1	0
NEW TECHNOLOGY AND PRODUCTS					
The introduction of new technology into the way you do your work	15	39	45	1	0
Changes in the work techniques or procedures that affect your job	9	29	59	2	1
The introduction of new products or services	13	30	56	0	0
ALTERATIONS TO THE 'DEAL'					
The proportion of your pay that is related to your performance	6	20	71	3	1
Changes in your working time arrangements	6	13	79	1	1

Note: Numbers are rounded and will therefore not always sum to 100 per cent.

' **Workers believe they are being asked to take on greater responsibilities and often more demanding work; they are being asked to do more.'**

while other organisational-level activity facilitates rather than inhibits workplace change.

Once again we can explore the impact of workplace change on attitudes and behaviour. We did this by taking the two main factors in Table 19. The impact of both types of change is generally positive. Change in job and work design is significantly associated with higher organisational commitment and work satisfaction and marginally significantly associated with improved employment relations and greater effort. Change in technology and products is associated with significantly lower intention to quit and marginally increased organisational commitment.

A second aspect of workplace change that was examined was a change of manager and the impact of this change. Rapid organisational change has the potential to disrupt working relationships and in particular to harm the psychological contract as managers who had made promises to their subordinates and built up a trusting relationship are moved on to other work. On some occasions it will be the workers who are moved, although in this study, we are interested only in those who have stayed in the same job in the same organisation during the past year. Of those in the same job, 29 per cent said their manager had changed in the last year, 35 per cent say they now have a better relationship with their new manager compared with the person who managed them a year ago, 20 per cent a worse relationship and 39 per cent say it is no different. The rest do not know. Among those who have the same manager, 70 per cent say their relationship is unchanged compared with a year ago. Of the remainder, 22 per cent say their relationship is better and only 6 per cent say it is worse. These results indicate that a change of immediate manager is a bit of a lottery, with sizeable numbers saying it has resulted in a better relationship and

somewhat smaller numbers reporting a worse relationship than a year ago. When we include those who have the same manager and look at changes in the relationship, the balance is slightly more positive suggesting that where there has been a change in the relationship, it is generally for the better.

Change in job content

We asked whether the job content or the way they do their job had changed in any way in the past year – 34 per cent said it had. This question is most relevant for those 493 in the sample who are in the same job as 12 months ago. A discriminant analysis revealed that those working for larger organisations were most likely to believe that the content of their jobs had changed. Among those whose job had changed, 37 per cent said it had become more challenging, interesting and/or responsible; 27 per cent said the job had become more demanding or the workload had increased; 9 per cent said it had been altered by new technology; 6 per cent said the job had been altered resulting in a new job description, and 4 per cent said that there had been an increase in team-working and working with others. On the more negative side, 4 per cent said the job had become less demanding but the workload had increased, implying some sort of de-skilling, and 3 per cent said the job had become less challenging and interesting.

For the great majority of those affected, the change in job content meant an increase in responsibility and challenge and/or an increase in demand and workload. The choice of language – whether to view an increase in the depth and breadth of the job as a challenge or a demand – may reflect differences in orientation to work. To explore this more fully, we undertook a discriminant analysis to identify those who did and did not refer to greater challenge. There was a tendency for those working in the public sector to view job change in terms of greater challenge, while those on fixed-term contracts were much less likely to cite greater challenges and responsibilities, presumably reflecting the constrained nature of the work allocated to them. However, the picture is rather more complex – when we undertake the same analysis among those who describe the changes as making the job more demanding, then we find that this kind of description is most likely to be made by those on fixed-term contracts; by implication, they in particular are likely to feel that they face increased demands and workload, with diminished responsibility and challenge. This raises some serious questions about the benefits of working on fixed-term contracts, bearing in mind that previous surveys have shown that they report a better psychological contract. In contrast to fixed-term contract workers, older workers are less likely than their younger counterparts to describe job changes in terms of increased demand. However, the general pattern is clear. Alongside the increase in working hours, the content of jobs is growing. Workers believe they are being asked to take on greater responsibilities and often more demanding work; they are being asked to do more.

On balance, workers favour these kinds of change. Asked whether the job is better, the same or worse than a year ago, 27 per cent said better, 11 per cent said worse while the remaining 62 per cent felt it was about the same. Among those who thought it was better:

◘ 49 per cent cited the increased challenge, interest and responsibility

◘ 11 per cent cited better rewards and prospects

◘ 10 per cent valued the increased team-working

◘ 9 per cent cited having more control over their job.

On the negative side, those saying their job had got worse over the year cited the increased demand and workload (39 per cent), poorer prospects and rewards (11 per cent) and poor management (11 per cent) as the reason for this.

These results confirm that there is a lot of change in job content – in what is sometimes termed functional flexibility. There is only a very small indication of de-skilling. There is considerable evidence that workers believe that their workload is being increased. For some this is viewed as a challenge, represented in increased responsibility and interest; for others it is a burden, reflected in a heavier and more demanding workload. We attempted to differentiate these two groups to identify any background characteristics associated with these different perceptions. In doing so, we should bear in mind that these might be different perceptions; they might also reflect genuine differences in what has been happening to jobs.

The final issue in exploring change in job content is to consider its consequences. We used the same kind of analysis as that adopted for analysis of other changes. This is a rigorous test, since it controls for all other factors over time that might have an impact on attitudes. The results show that change in job content has no significant independent impact on attitudes towards work. However, it does have a negative impact on effort together with a positive impact on innovation behaviour. Since most changes reflect increased autonomy and control, what this seems to imply is that if workers are given greater control over their work, they believe this results in reduced amounts of effort required and increased capacity to innovate. It is important to bear in mind that effort, as contrasted with our measure of motivation, is generally regarded by workers as negative and is considered to be a function of external pressures rather than internal drive. By implication, the impact of change in job content is generally benign.

Changes in personnel policies

We have already examined the experience of human resource practices and noted how these have altered over the year. A separate set of questions asked more explicitly about changes in personnel policies that might affect them. Among the 493 in the same jobs, 22 per cent said that there had been changes. These changes have been fairly evenly spread across the main areas of personnel policy. Of those reporting a change:

- 42 per cent said there had been changes in policies affecting security, training, prospects or careers

- 40 per cent cited changes in policies affecting rewards, pay or appraisal

- 34 per cent mentioned changes in policy affecting information, communication, involvement and relationships

- 33 per cent mentioned policies affecting how, when and where work is done

- 9 per cent thought there had been changes but they either could not specify what they were or felt they fell outside the categories listed above.

These results indicate that important changes in personnel policy have affected just over one-fifth of workers who have remained in the same jobs over the year. There is no clear pattern to the type of change and in a few cases there appears to have been a major overhaul of personnel policy with changes over a number of areas. However, compared to the 49 per cent who reported organisational change and the numbers reporting workplace change, the amount of reported change in personnel policies seems to be relatively modest.

We explored whether change in personnel policies was likely to have taken place in particular contexts. It was no more likely in one sector than another but was significantly more likely to be reported by those working in larger establishments. This may be partly a reflection of the fact that larger establishments are more likely to have a well-developed personnel function and set of personnel policies.

We can also examine the consequences of change in personnel policy, remembering that only a little more than one in five reported such change in the previous year. The standard analysis of change over time reveals that changes to personnel policies had no significant impact on work behaviour but did affect attitudes. In particular, personnel policy changes had a negative impact in leading to poorer employment relations and lowered levels of job security. When we look more closely at these results, the negative impact on employment relations can be attributed to the changes in policy affecting how, when and where the work is done while, more surprisingly, lowered job security is associated with policy changes in the area of information, communication, involvement or relationships. The results came quite close to

> 'Workplace changes in job design and new technology and products is
> generally welcomed, but changes in personnel policies have a more
> negative effect, especially on job security and employment relations.'

statistical significance on a number of other outcomes and in each case were negative. This indicates that, whether through the process whereby they are introduced or the content of the changes, personnel policy changes have a negative impact. Such consistent findings suggest that policy changes should not be introduced lightly and that much thought should be given to the process whereby they are introduced.

Attitudes to change at work

Change has been shown to be pervasive and has generally had a bad press. However, the analysis so far indicates that much depends on the type of change and points to the need for a more subtle and focused analysis. In this final section on change, we explore attitudes to change at work to determine whether change was generally viewed in a negative light and to see how far it was possible to differentiate between those who viewed change as more positive or negative.

Several items explored attitudes to change. We conducted a factor analysis to see whether they hang together to form either a single scale or a set of scales. In the event, it was not possible to identify any useful groupings. The items are shown in Table 20.

The responses in Table 20 provide an antidote to those who argue that change is viewed negatively. Over 60 per cent disagree that there is too much change going on where they work and that they feel anxious when changes happen at work. Over 60 per cent also believe that on balance changes make things better rather than worse. A large majority similarly believe they can participate in and contribute to change. There is a sub-group of no more than about 10 per cent who feel anxious and concerned about the amount of change at work. But for a majority, change is not a major matter of concern and is seen as a necessary and often positive part of organisational life.

Table 20 | Attitudes to change

% (n = 493)	strongly agree	agree	disagree	strongly disagree
There is too much change going on in the place where I work	11	27	50	11
I feel anxious when changes happen at work	7	32	48	13
On the whole, changes at work make things better rather than worse	9	52	26	4
We all have to learn to live with change	38	59	3	0
Workers are expected to come up with ideas for change	10	54	28	6
I can participate in, contribute to or help to shape changes that affect me at work	17	64	14	4
Workers should be able to participate in all changes that directly affect them	43	52	5	0

Note: Numbers are rounded and will therefore not always sum to 100 per cent.

We examined the results in more detail to identify those who were more or less positive about change at work. Since the items did not work as a scale, we took the first item in Table 20, which reflects a general view about change at work, and looked to see who responded more or less positively, focusing on background characteristics and experience of practices in 1998 and excluding attitudes. Those most likely to say that there is too much change going on work in larger organisations and are more likely to be older and to be trade union members. Those who disagreed with this view had more scope for direct participation in their work, worked in service and support jobs and, at a marginal level of significance, included those on higher incomes and those on fixed-term contracts. We should be cautious about reading too much into the analysis of this single item, but it does appear to confirm that anxiety about change is perceived as most acute among older workers in large organisations and is ameliorated by the experience of direct participation.

Summary

The results in this chapter confirm that there is a large amount of change taking place in organisations. This change is generally accepted as an inevitable part of organisational life and often welcomed. Only a minority of older workers in larger organisations appear to feel threatened by too much change. The consequences of change depend partly on the type of change. Large amounts of organisational change have a negative impact on attitudes but the most consistently negative attitudes are associated with redundancy programmes, while technological change has

generally positive outcomes. Workplace changes in job design and new technology and products is generally welcomed, but changes in personnel policies have a more negative effect, especially on job security and employment relations. It may be that the level at which change takes place has an important impact. Organisational-level changes and personnel policy changes, which are likely to occur at organisational level, tend to have a more negative impact while local changes, which might be more easily understood and controlled, appear to be positively received. In general, the study finds no evidence of a widespread antipathy to change at work unless there is too much of it going on at once; on the contrary, the benefits to individuals are sometimes believed to outweigh the costs.

5 | Violations of the psychological contract

◘ **Although promises made by the organisation are quite frequently broken, this seems to be accepted as an inevitable part of working life. Serious violations of the psychological contract are relatively rare.**

◘ **Serious violations of the psychological contract have an emotional impact, reflected in reactions such as annoyance, betrayal, anger and hurt.**

◘ **The most serious violation of the psychological contract admitted by workers is a reduction in their effort.**

As we have previously noted, part of the reason for the renewed interest in the psychological contract in recent years is the belief that changes in organisations have resulted in a breakdown of traditional relationships and in unfulfilled expectations. In short, organisational change leads to violation of the traditional psychological contract. However, this is an assertion supported by anecdotes about changes in career opportunities and lowered job security. Our own surveys have challenged the evidence about low levels of job security. What about violation of the psychological contract? Is this a reality?

To explore this issue, we adopted two perspectives. The first was to determine whether and for what reasons individuals felt that their psychological contract had been violated by the organisation in the previous year. Second, we turned the issue around to examine how far workers would acknowledge that they too violated their side of the psychological contract. In considering the results, we should bear in mind that many workers reported that they engaged in a variety of positive behaviours, such as offering suggestions for innovation at work or engaging in organisational citizenship behaviours that go beyond their defined role.

Violation by the organisation

Interviewees were asked whether the organisation had broken any important promises or commitments to them in the past year. We should bear in mind that a set of questions reported earlier in our core analysis of the psychological contract asked about the extent to which the organisation had kept its promises and commitments in a range of specified areas. In general, less than 10 per cent felt that the organisation had completely failed to keep its promises and commitments in each area, although rather more were agreed that they had gone only some of the way towards keeping them. The exception was help in dealing with problems encountered outside work, where 11 per cent said that the organisation had completely failed to keep its promises and commitments.

In the event, only 12 per cent said the organisation had broken an important promise or commitment in the past year. Although quite a wide range of issues were cited, most fell into a few areas: 36 per cent said the promises concerned pay and benefits and 19 per cent mentioned promotion. These were followed by working environment (8 per cent), training and development (7 per cent),

> ' ... workers feel more strongly about violation when they believe managers are to blame, either as a result of deliberate actions or through incompetence.'

job security (7 per cent) and workload (7 per cent). Other items concerned general treatment described in terms of fairness, recognition and respect. Looking back to the earlier results, 8 per cent said that the organisation had failed to keep its promises with respect to pay and also in relation to careers.

A discriminant analysis was undertaken to determine who was more likely to report a violation by the organisation. Based on the 1999 responses, those more likely to report a violation had fewer educational qualifications, worked in larger organisations and experienced fewer human resource practices but had higher levels of direct participation. This last item is possibly the most unexpected. One explanation might be that those with greater autonomy are more likely to have this autonomy and the decision-making that goes with it challenged by higher echelons of the organisation. By using the various background, policy and practice variables, it was possible to predict correctly who would be more likely to report a violation 87 per cent of the time.

One of the issues in exploring violations by the organisation concerns who represents the organisation. Indeed, since pay and benefits and promotion are often cited, it might be thought that the personnel department might attract the 'blame'. We asked who broke the promise: 44 per cent said senior management, 24 per cent mentioned their line manager and 22 per cent just referred to the organisation itself as an abstract entity. Only 3 per cent cited another department in the organisation, implying that perhaps personnel departments, unless they are associated with the anonymous organisation in the abstract, are not being blamed. Support from this might come from the relatively low levels of perceived change in personnel policies.

So if management is largely to blame, why did it do it? The most widely cited explanation was that it had no choice – 39 per cent said that their management could not control the event. On the other hand, 22 per cent cited incompetence and 22 per cent felt that they had been deliberately misled and that the management had never intended to keep the promise in the first place. A further 11 per cent cited the pressure and workload that managers were under. From this we can see that about half of those who complained about violation of promises offer a benevolent attribution and just under half are more critical of management competence and motives. Confirming this, 43 per cent felt that those considered to have broken the promise could be held personally responsible, while 53 per cent felt they were influenced by factors beyond their control. The rest were uncertain. In parallel with this, 44 per cent felt that the violation was deliberate, while 47 per cent thought it was unintentional. There is therefore a sub-set who attribute to management and the organisation fairly Machiavellian motives, concerned with deliberately misleading by making false promises and then breaking them.

We can take this analysis just a little further by identifying which of the explanatory factors is most strongly associated with a feeling of violation. This shows that where the manager is viewed as incompetent, personally responsible and where there had been a deliberate attempt to mislead, then the sense of violation was greater. Not surprisingly, workers feel more strongly about violation when they believe managers are to blame, either as a result of deliberate actions or through incompetence.

By implication, there are some strong emotions involved in the experience of violation of aspects of the psychological contract. This was explored and is summarised in Table 21.

The results in Table 21 indicate that emotions associated with violation run quite high. The main emotion is annoyance, coupled with anger and a sense of betrayal. Interestingly the outcome is often not much of a surprise, suggesting that this may be part of a pattern of behaviour and related expectations. Finally, there is very little sympathy for those responsible for the violation, even if it was beyond their control.

Violation by employees

In much of the analysis of change and violation of the psychological contract, the emphasis has been placed on violation by the organisation. The assumption has been that workers might engage in withdrawal behaviours such as reduced commitment, lower levels of motivation and citizenship behaviour and perhaps an increased propensity to leave the organisation. Rather less

attention has been placed on conscious and deliberate acts by workers that they may well acknowledge as constituting violation of what the organisation expects of them but which the worker may feel justified in undertaking as part of the altered effort–reward bargain. We therefore explored the extent to which workers reported that they engaged in a range of activities that might be considered by the organisation to be a violation of the psychological contract.

A number of items that might reflect violation of the psychological contract were presented to the whole sample of those in employment. Since these items are being used for the first time, the results were factor analysed to see whether they fell into distinct groups. This analysis produced four factors, which are presented in Table 22.

Most people will admit that they have criticised either their boss or their organisation on some occasions. Rather fewer accept that they have avoided responsibilities or commitments, with the

Table 21 | Emotions associated with violation of the psychological contract

% (n=72)	not at all	a little	somewhat	a lot
TO WHAT EXTENT DID YOU EXPERIENCE THE FOLLOWING FEELINGS IN RELATION TO THE INCIDENT?				
Annoyance	3	11	19	67
Betrayal	21	15	18	46
Anger	14	25	17	44
Surprise	50	13	10	28
Hurt	35	21	11	33
Understanding/sympathy for the other party	60	26	7	7

The alpha scores for the four factors were .58, .50, .69 and .23 respectively. These are rather lower than we might expect for well-validated measures, but they do suggest that with the exception of the final factor, the factors hang together sufficiently to be considered as separate sets of items.

Note: Numbers are rounded and will therefore not always sum to 100 per cent.

exception of sometimes keeping other people waiting. Most have thought about leaving the organisation. We did not undertake a full statistical analysis of abuse of privileges, and the low levels of reported abuse may reflect low access to computers and telephones. However, it is interesting to note that on the basis of descriptive results, it is managers – who may have greatest access – who are most likely to admit to abuse of these privileges. More generally, we must be aware

of the possibility that some people may be reluctant to admit that they engage in anti-social behaviour and the responses may therefore be an underestimate of the actual amount of psychological contract violation by employees.

With these limitations in mind, we can go one step further and identify the sort of people who are more likely to admit to violating their side of the psychological contract and the policies and

Table 22 | Violation of the psychological contract by employees

	never	rarely	sometimes	often
CRITICAL COMMENT				
Criticised your boss behind his/her back	32	15	29	23
Criticised the organisation to people outside work	39	22	26	13
Done the minimum you can get away with	57	23	16	4
AVOIDED RESPONSIBILITIES/COMMITMENTS				
Kept others waiting for things you should have finished earlier	55	34	10	1
Passed on to others things you should really have had responsibility for	70	24	5	0
Worked at your full capacity in all your job duties	2	3	19	76
Refused reasonable requests for help from more senior staff	82	13	4	1
Had a day off sick when you were well enough to go to work	79	16	4	0
CONSIDERED JOBS ELSEWHERE				
Looked for job advertisements in newspapers to which you could apply	29	20	28	23
Seriously considered leaving the organisation	37	20	26	16
ABUSE OF PRIVILEGES				
Surfed the Internet for things unrelated to work	69	5	9	7
Gone beyond what you understand to be an acceptable use of your office telephone for personal calls	54	21	14	5

Note: Numbers are rounded and will therefore not always sum to 100 per cent.

'Most workers admit that on occasion they violate their side of the psychological contract.'

attitudes associated with this violation. We can do this through a regression analysis on the three scales covering dimensions of violation for which we had reasonable data.

Looking first at the relatively modest form of violation reflected in making critical comments, the 1999 data show that those who are younger, those who report poorer employment relations, those with lower levels of organisational commitment and those with higher levels of direct participation are more likely to make critical comments. The first two of these items, namely being younger and experiencing poorer employment relations are also predictors of this sort of violation based on the 1998 data, suggesting that they are quite powerful determinants of such behaviour. The various background factors explain 23 per cent of the variation in responses based on 1999 data and 11 per cent based on 1998 responses.

The second set of violation items is concerned with avoiding responsibilities and commitments. Using both the 1998 and the 1999 data, only age predicts this kind of violation. Younger workers are more likely to say they deliberately avoid responsibilities at work. However, even the 1999 data explain only 7 per cent of the variation in responses.

The third type of violation concerns considering jobs elsewhere. Like the others, it is a relatively mild form of 'violation'. Based on the 1999 data, those more likely to consider a job elsewhere are those with a shorter tenure, a poorer psychological contract, a job at management level, lower levels of work satisfaction and poorer employment relations. Together these explain 32 per cent of the variation in responses. Using the 1998 data and explaining 17 per cent of the variation in

responses, the first three listed above predict whether or not employees have been considering a job elsewhere, suggesting that they are the key influences on such behaviour. As we might expect, there is some overlap between the influences identified here and those associated with a stronger intention to leave the job.

Summary

Violation of the psychological contract by the employer affects only a minority of workers. However, when it does occur it is usually considered to be a serious issue and is most likely to be concerned with pay and benefits and with promotion. Minor day-to-day violations are almost inevitable in any work setting; however, only 11 per cent identified important violations in the past year. Usually these were attributed either to senior or line management and, if linked to perceived incompetence or deceit, they resulted in strong emotions of annoyance, betrayal and anger. In other words, when they occur, they are important.

Most workers admit that on occasion they violate their side of the psychological contract. But few do so often and many claim never to let it affect their work performance. Of course, their managers might take a rather different view.

We had some success in identifying who was more likely to report that their psychological contract had been violated and who had engaged in such violation themselves.

6 | Conclusions and policy implications

◻ **The best way to ensure a positive psychological contract is to ensure that a set of progressive human resource practices are in place, along with a supportive and participative organisational climate.**

◻ **Change in the psychological contract causes a change in key attitudes and behaviour. Therefore, more attention needs to be paid to the effective application of human resource management.**

◻ **Contrary to some predictions, change has not destroyed the psychological contract. Carefully managed, change can even enhance it.**

◻ **Change appears to be much less of a threat to the psychological contract than bad management.**

The theme of the 1999 survey of the state of the employment relationship was change at work. We examined this in two main ways. First, we obtained information over time from a sample who were previously interviewed in 1998 to enable us to track changes in attitude and behaviour and to determine the causes of any changes. Second, we examined the experience of and attitudes towards change including change of work, reflected in obtaining a new job, and change at work, reflected in changes in the organisation and in the workplace. In addition, we looked more closely at violation of the psychological contract. Underpinning this interest in change was an awareness that change at work has had a bad press. It has been widely argued that there is too much unnecessary change causing stress and dissatisfaction among the workforce. Changes at work have also been cited as the main reason for the breakdown in the traditional psychological contract, leading to widespread violations of that contract by the organisation and possibly by workers.

Our previous surveys have led us to be somewhat sceptical about such claims. We have found that the workforce is relatively secure, satisfied and

motivated. The psychological contract is in fairly good shape. We could describe the state of the employment relationship as generally positive. Of course, each year we have identified a minority, often on the margins of employment, who are much less satisfied and secure and we have drawn attention to their serious concerns. But they represent no more than about 20 per cent of the workforce we have surveyed. On this basis, it appears that the damage to the psychological contract and the employment relationship of developments at work have been exaggerated. Shall we find the same with respect to the experience of change? This is what we set out to explore.

This is the first in the CIPD annual series of surveys where we have obtained information from the same people in two successive years. On previous occasions we have selected a random sample to ensure that we can present results that are representative of the workforce as a whole. This year, our inability to re-interview everyone means that the sample may be slightly less representative. But this is more than compensated for by our ability to make much more confident statements about causal links. In the past we have been able

> ' The psychological contract is in fairly good shape. We
> could describe the state of the employment relationship
> as generally positive.'

to show an association between, say, the
psychological contract and employee commitment
to the organisation and we might infer that one
leads to the other. By looking at information about
the psychological contract in 1998 and examining
its impact on commitment in 1999, we can be
more confident that a positive psychological
contract is a cause of high commitment.

The state of the psychological contract

Looking at changes over time can place heavy
demands on the data. If we take a construct such
as organisational commitment, one of its

characteristics is that it is intended to be stable.
We should therefore not expect much change over
a year. If there is not much change to explain, this
means that any background variables that appear
to predict such changes at a satisfactory level of
statistical significance really must be important.
On this basis, what have we found? The
longitudinal changes are summarised in Figure 9.
Each link shows where practices or behaviour in
1998 predicted changes between 1998 and 1999.
We can see that background factors have only
a limited ability to predict the state of the
psychological contract. However, the state of
the psychological contract in 1998 predicts all the

Figure 9 | Changes between 1998 and 1999 (all results show how 1998 responses predict those for 1999)

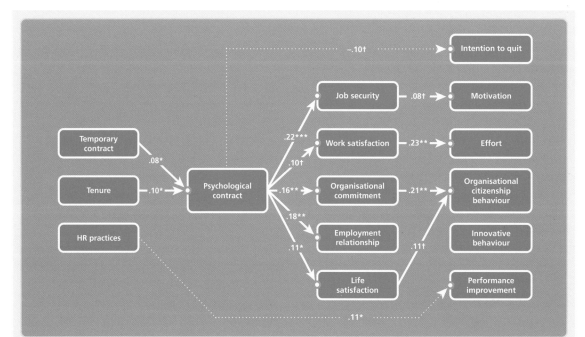

Note

1 The diagram is a summary of a large number of separate regression analyses and should be read from left to right as follows: the first set of
links are between 1998 background factors and change in the psychological contract between 1998 and 1999; the next set of links are
between 1998 ratings of the psychological contract and changes in attitudes between 1998 and 1999; the final set of links in the model
represent 1998 ratings of attitudes and changes in behaviour between 1998 and 1999.

2 † slightly different; * significant; ** strongly significant; ***very strongly significant.

' ... if you want a positive psychological contract, then it is
important to invest in human resource practices and to
foster a climate of direct participation.'

core attitudes we measured in 1999. These
attitudes in turn show a modest ability to predict
various aspects of behaviour. In addition,
experience of more of the high commitment
human resource practices in 1998 is associated
with higher ratings of improved performance in
1999. This is shown with a broken line since it is
stronger than any effect through the psychological
contract and attitudes. Similarly, the psychological
contract shows a stronger link to lower intention
to quit than any of the attitudinal items. Because
of the impact over time, the summary in Figure 9
represents quite a powerful set of results.

One of the consistent findings is that changes are
better explained by looking at current practices
rather than those of a year ago. For example, the
human resource practices in place in 1999 predict
changes between 1998 and 1999 in the
psychological contract better than the human
resource practices in place in 1998. This is not
surprising. When the 1999 survey was conducted,
many workers would be reacting to the practices in
place at that time and which, by implication, had
been introduced some time in the past. If we bring
together the results of current significant
associations between the key variables, then the
core model of the role of the psychological contract
stands up well. This can be seen in Figure 10.

Figure 10 | Changes between 1998 and 1999 (all results show how 1999 responses explain changes between 1998 and 1999)

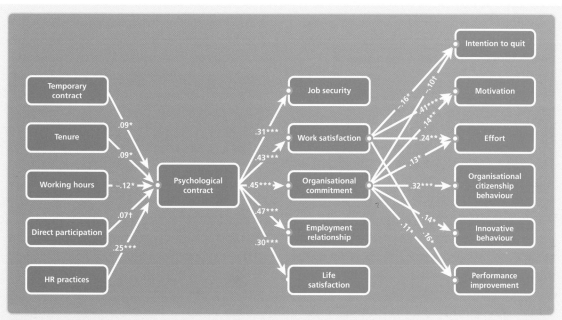

Note

1 The figure shows statistically significant links within the core model. In each case, they report how responses in 1999 explain changes in
   other variables between 1998 and 1999. There will be a separate direct effect on 1999 outcomes that is not shown here. This figure also
   omits additional links, for example between HR practices and performance or direct participation and innovative behaviour, which are
   shown in the main report.

2 † slightly significant; * significant; ** strongly significant; *** very strongly significant.

Policy implications

The findings in Figures 9 and 10 have a number of important policy implications. First and foremost, they suggest that if you want a positive psychological contract, then it is important to invest in human resource practices and to foster a climate of direct participation. The reason why this makes sense is that a positive psychological contract is in turn associated with a range of positive attitudes that link through to positive behaviour. Even allowing for a certain amount of caution about some of the measures, we can trace a link to high levels of motivation, performance improvement, more co-operation and innovation, and a greater likelihood of staying with the organisation. In some cases, such as performance improvement, there is also a more direct link from human resource practices.

So much for the good news. On the basis of previous surveys, attitudes to work improved slightly, year by year, between 1996 and 1998. In 1999 this trend has been reversed. On most measures, responses in 1999 are slightly more negative than in 1998. In a number of cases this downward trend reaches statistical significance. There may be reasons for this that lie outside the scope of the survey, but some of the explanation can be found within it.

There is evidence in the survey of a decline in the use of human resource practices and in the climate and scope for direct participation. Since both of these are strongly associated, directly or indirectly, with many of the outcomes, an apparent change in management practice is probably having a damaging impact. This survey, in line with others about which the CIPD has published reports – including the Workplace Employee Relations Survey (WERS) and the Birkbeck Future of Work Survey (Guest *et al*, 2000a, 2000b) – reveals that managers are reluctant to invest in the kind of human resource practices that have consistently been shown to have a positive impact. It is notable in this survey that one of the steepest declines is in the use of employee involvement and quality programmes. These may have fallen out of fashion and seem rather passé to some managers, but there was strong evidence from WERS that these often informal attempts to increase employee involvement were linked to greater employee commitment. Apparently the penny has not yet dropped.

Another factor that may have contributed to a decline in satisfaction is the continuing rise in the demands of work (about half said they had to work harder than a year ago), particularly for those in senior management positions. There is a paradox in that those we might expect to have most control over their work are the most overworked. One reason may be that they are reluctant to delegate. The groups recording the largest drops in scope for direct participation were middle managers and blue-collar workers. Top management may be too busy pursuing other priorities to find the time to create space for themselves and others by delegating and by paying attention to the creation and management of an appropriate organisational culture based on serious investment in human resource management and employee involvement.

Despite this slightly worrying downward trend, it is important to emphasise that most workers remain satisfied, committed and motivated. Most are broadly content with the state of their psychological contract. But if the decline in the use of the kind of key practices that make a difference

'Change is both pervasive and generally positive. The model of the psychological contract, linking human resource practices to a range of outcomes, remains robust.'

continues, we can expect to see further rises in dissatisfaction and disaffection, with negative consequences for consequent performance at work.

Change at work

The evidence from these workers confirms that change at work is now the norm: 6 per cent have moved out of employment in the past year and 9.7 per cent have changed their employer. A number of others have moved within the same organisation or have changed their employment status from a temporary or fixed-term contract to something else. However, most of this change has been voluntary and the great majority of those who have moved feel that the change was a good thing and that they are now better off than they were a year ago. In other words, change in employment has been a positive experience, not a source of major anxiety and insecurity.

A majority of those who have stayed in the same job over the year have also experienced some sort of change. The most pervasive has been organisational change. Even over a single year, a striking 49 per cent reported that their organisation had been going through a major change programme. These changes included mergers and acquisitions, redundancies, restructuring, workplace reorganisation, new technology systems and culture change. In some cases all of these had been experienced. Where large amounts of change of different sorts – defined as four or more of the six changes listed above – had been occurring, the effects tended to be negative. The changes did not seem to affect performance, but they left workers feeling less secure, less content with employment relations, less motivated and less satisfied with life as a

whole. We should not be surprised that mass organisational change is not good for workers. However, closer inspection revealed that we should not brand all organisational change as negative. If we view specific types of change in isolation, then redundancy programmes stand out as particularly negative. In contrast, technology changes were more likely to have positive effects. The impact of most other types of change was broadly neutral. It is interesting to note that policies intended to guarantee no redundancies reflect the single significant area of increase among the human resource practices between 1998 and 1999. The policy implications are clear. Organisations should avoid redundancy programmes if at all possible. They give off strong negative signals to remaining employees, damaging their satisfaction, security and motivation.

Changes in the workplace were also quite common and were sometimes linked, inevitably, to organisational change. Typical changes fell into two distinctive areas concerned with job content and new technology. Close to half of the sample reported some sort of increase in work responsibilities and demands, and a slightly smaller proportion reported changes in the specific technology in their workplace. Despite the increased workloads and responsibilities, the impact of these workplace changes is generally positive, leading to higher work satisfaction, higher commitment and lower likelihood of leaving the organisation. On balance, the experience of workplace change is reported as positive rather than negative. The same general pattern holds true for specific changes in job content – 34 per cent said their job content had changed over the previous year, mainly resulting in increased responsibilities and challenges or increased demands. The choice of language may reflect reactions to the change. Although change in job content has little impact on attitudes and behaviour, 27 per cent said their job was now better compared with 11 per cent who said it was worse. This still leaves a large majority who had experienced change in job content who reported that the job felt about the same. In summary, job change has a modest positive impact on workers. The same can be said for another change we examined – change of boss. This affected 29 per cent of the workers in the sample and was generally seen as positive rather than negative.

Change in personnel policy

The only sour note with respect to change occurs when we look at change in personnel policy, although only 22 per cent reported that they were affected by it in the past year. More specifically, changes affecting how, when and where work can be carried out had a strong negative impact on both employment relations and job security, and change in personnel policy in general tended to have a more modest but negative impact on a range of other attitudes. These personnel changes may be associated with larger organisational changes, but there are policy lessons here. Whether through the content or the way in which they were introduced, changes in personnel policy have a more negative impact than any kind of change other than a redundancy programme. Changes in personnel policy should therefore not be entered into lightly.

Leaving aside the slightly negative tone of the personnel changes, the broad pattern of results contradicts the popular impression that change is invariably painful and damaging to morale. This is reinforced when we examine attitudes towards change in general. Over 60 per cent disagree that there is too much change going on where they work or that change at work leads to anxiety. A huge majority agree that they have to live with change. In other words, change has become a normal, accepted and often positive part of life at work. Many changes are viewed as positive and it is only when change becomes overwhelming, or specific types of change, such as redundancy or certain kinds of personnel policy change, are introduced that reactions become more negative.

Violation of the psychological contract

The final issue examined in the survey was violation of the psychological contract. Violation is a strong word and only 12 per cent admitted to violation by the organisation, reflected in the breaking of important promises. Senior or line management was usually held responsible and where the broken promise was attributed to either incompetence, personal responsibility or deliberate deceit, then there were strong negative emotional reactions associated with it. Most employees admit that they occasionally break their side of the psychological contract, mainly in the form of covert criticism or considering alternative jobs. But most deny any serious attempt to reduce performance and contribution and the activities they admit to rarely amount to what most would regard as serious violation.

Summary

This study finds that change is both pervasive and generally positive. It also finds that the model of the psychological contract, linking human resource practices to a range of outcomes, remains robust. The problem is that management is sometimes failing to provide the necessary input to the model in the form of progressive human resource practices and a climate of involvement and partnership.

References

CULLY M., O'REILLY A., WOODLAND S. AND DIX S. (1999)

Britain at Work: As depicted by the 1998 Workplace Employee Relations Survey. London, Routledge.

GUEST D. AND CONWAY N. (1999)

How Dissatisfied Are British Workers? London, Institute of Personnel and Development.

GUEST D., MICHIE J., SHEEHAN M. AND CONWAY N. (2000A)

Employment Relations, HRM and Business Performance. London, Institute of Personnel and Development.

GUEST D., MICHIE J., SHEEHAN M., CONWAY N. AND METOCHI M. (2000B)

Effective People Management: Initial findings of the Future of Work Study. London, Chartered Institute of Personnel and Development.

Appendix 1

Descriptive summary of background variables in 1999 (n=582)

Background variable	Category	Percentage of sample
Number of employees at same location	Fewer than 10 employees	13.3
	10–24 employees	18.8
	25–99 employees	26.7
	100–499 employees	25.1
	500–999 employees	8.0
	1,000 or more employees	8.0
Total number of employees in organisation	10–24 employees	10.0
	25–99 employees	14.6
	100–499 employees	13.7
	500–999 employees	7.9
	1,000 or more employees	53.8
Type of industry	Chemical	0.7
	Construction	3.2
	Consumer products	1.9
	Financial services	5.4
	Food and drink	6.3
	General manufacturing	9.5
	High tech/electronics	3.9
	Hotel and leisure	2.3
	Media/broadcasting	1.6
	Oil/mining	0.7
	Paper and packaging	0.7
	Pharmaceutical	1.1
	Professional services	13.2
	Publishing/printing	1.4
	Retailing	8.1
	Transportation and distribution	5.1
	Utilities (water, gas, electric)	1.6
	Health	9.8
	Local government	12.7
	Central government (including defence)	1.9
	Other services	9.0
Contract of employment	Temporary	5.6
	Fixed-term	7.7
	Permanent	86.8
Type of job	Managers and administrators (eg store/shop/sales manager, office or facility manager)	15.3
	Professional (eg doctor, lawyer, chartered accountant, teacher, architect, social worker)	17.2
	Associate professional or technical (e.g. technician, nurse, building inspector, computer programmer, musician)	12.2
	Clerical/secretarial (eg typist, postal clerk, secretary, telephone operator, computer operator, bank clerk)	16.3

Background variable	Category	Percentage of sample
	Craft (eg bricklayer, tool maker, electrician, fitter, motor mechanic)	5.7
	Personal and protective (eg police officer, bar staff, hairdresser, undertaker)	10.5
	Sales (eg buyer, sales assistant, sales representative, credit agent)	7.9
	Plant/machine operator (eg assembly line worker, truck driver, taxi or bus driver)	9.6
	Other occupation	5.3
Whether part of management of the organisation	Upper management	7.1
	Middle management	23.2
	Lower management	14.9
	Non-manager	54.8
Actual hours worked in a typical week in main job	10 or less	2.1
	11–20	8.6
	21–30	10.9
	31–40	40.9
	41–50	27.5
	51+	10.0
Tenure	5 years or less	40.0
	Between 5 and 10 years	28.2
	Between 10 and 20 years	18.7
	More than 20 years	13.1
Age	18–24	8.2
	25–29	16.3
	30–34	15.3
	35–44	27.3
	45–54	24.2
	55–65	8.6
Trade union or staff association membership	Yes	40.0
	No	60.0
Highest educational qualification	CSE/GCSE (grades D–G)/NVQ level 1	7.9
	O level/GCSE (grades A–C)/NVQ level 2	23.4
	A levels/NVQ level 3	20.7
	Degree or equivalent	26.2
	Postgraduate or equivalent	6.9
	No formal qualifications	14.8
Sex	Male	49.7
	Female	50.3

Background variable	Category	Percentage of sample
Average gross pay	Less than £111 per week	11.4
	£111 – £130 per week	3.5
	£131 – £150 per week	4.6
	£151 – £170 per week	2.2
	£171 – £190 per week	2.9
	£191 – £230 per week	9.6
	£231 – £270 per week	11.8
	£271 – £340 per week	13.6
	£341 – £420 per week	13.6
	£421 – £500 per week	13.4
	£501 – £600 per week	5.3
	£601 or more per week	7.9
Number of children of school age or younger	0	55.2
	1	17.9
	2	20.5
	3	4.5
	4	1.4
	5 or more	0.5
Marital status	Single	24.4
	Married or living as married	64.8
	Separated/divorced	9.3
	Widowed	1.5
Status of earner within household	All of the income	37.6
	Most of the income	21.6
	Half of the income	18.8
	Less than half of the income	22.1

Appendix 2

Measurement of variables

The tables below describe how the variables used in the path analysis were constructed from items contained in the survey questionnaire.

Table A1 | Construction of measures used in core analysis in Chapter 2

Variable name	Variable type[1]	Description
BACKGROUND VARIABLES		
Company size	Interval	Single item, ranging from 2=10–24 employees to 6=1,000 or more employees.
Establishment size	Interval	Single item, ranging from 1=fewer than 10 employees to 6=1,000 or more employees.
Type of industry	Dummy	Two dummy variables were used to represent type of industry:
		1. Whether the business was in the public (coded 1) or private sector (coded 0).
		2. Whether the business came from the industrial sector (coded 1) or not (coded 0). Industrial sector here includes chemical, high tech/electronics, oil/mining, paper and packaging, pharmaceutical, and the utilities (water, gas, electric). Other sectors are shown in Appendix 1.
Type of contract	Dummy	Two dummy variables were used to represent type of contract:
		1. Whether the respondent was employed on a fixed-term contract (coded 1) or not (coded 0).
		2. Whether the respondent was employed on a temporary contract (coded 1) or not (coded 0).
Type of job	Dummy	Three dummy variables were used to represent job type:
		1. Whether the jobs could be classified as being broadly 'blue-collar' jobs (coded 1) or not (coded 0). 'Blue-collar' jobs here refers to crafts or plant/machine operators categories.
		2. Whether the jobs could be classified as being broadly 'white-collar' jobs (coded 1) or not (coded 0). 'White-collar' jobs here refers to associate professional and technical or clerical/secretarial categories.
		3 Whether the jobs could be classified as being services (coded 1) or not (coded 0). Services here refers to personal and protective or sales categories.
Union membership	Dummy	Whether respondent reported belonging to a recognised trade union or staff association (yes=1, no=0).
Age	Interval	6-point scale, ranging from 1=18–24 to 6=55–65.
Gender	Dummy	Male=1, Female=0
Education	Interval	6-point scale, ranging from 0=no formal qualifications to 5=postgraduate or equivalent.
Income	Interval	12-point scale ranging from 1=less than £111 per week/less than £5,721 per year, to 12=£601 or more per week/£31,201 or more per year.

Table A1 | Continued

Variable name	Variable type[1]	Description
Management level	Interval	4-point scale ranging from 1=non-manager to 4=upper manager.
Length of service	Interval	Measured in years.
Number of hours worked	Interval	Measured by number of hours worked.
ANTECEDENTS		
HR practices	Interval	This variable is a count across 10 items assessing HR practices. For each of the 10 items, participants were asked whether a particular aspect of HR applied in their organisation (coded 1) or not (coded 0). The 10 aspects of HR practices assessed were: the provision of interesting work; avoiding compulsory redundancy; internal recruitment; involvement practices; opportunities for training; kept informed on how well the company is doing; equal opportunity practices; family-friendly policies; formal performance appraisals; and performance-related pay. Alpha=0.65.
Direct participation	Interval	4 items asking respondents the extent to which they agree with statements surrounding participation in the design of their work (eg 'I vary how I do my work?'). Alpha=0.83.
THE PSYCHOLOGICAL CONTRACT		
Psychological contract	Interval	9 items assessing the extent to which the respondent feels the organisation has kept its promises (6 items), treated them fairly (1 item), and how much they trust the organisation (2 items). Alpha=0.86.
OUTCOMES		
Commitment	Interval	2 items (eg 'How much loyalty would you say you feel towards the organisation you work for as a whole?'). Alpha=0.73.
Life satisfaction	Interval	6 items (eg 'How satisfied are you with your life as a whole these days?'). Alpha=0.77.
Work satisfaction	Interval	Single item ('How satisfied are you with your work?').
Security	Interval	Single item ('How secure do you feel in your present job?').
Employment relations	Interval	Single item ('Overall, how would you rate relations between employees and management at your organisation?').
Effort	Interval	Single item ('In your present job, how much of the time are you working really hard?').
Motivation	Interval	2 items (eg 'How motivated do you feel in your present job?'). Alpha=0.58.

Table A1 | Continued

Variable name	Variable type[1]	Description
Obligation to perform organisational citizenship behaviours	Interval	4 items (eg 'How obliged do you feel to volunteer to do tasks outside your job description?'). Alpha=0.70.
Intention to quit	Interval	Single item ('Have you ever thought about or done anything about trying to leave your current job?').
Innovation	Interval	3 items. Respondents were asked the extent to which they made innovative suggestions (eg 'I make innovative suggestions to help improve my department.'). Alpha=0.67.
Performance	Interval	Single item ('How would you rate your own performance at work now compared with a year ago?').

1. Variables used in multiple regression are required to be either interval variables or dummy variables. Interval variables are variables where the intervals between the categories are identical and the categories can be ordered in terms of 'more' and 'less' of the concept in question (for example age, satisfaction, commitment, etc). Dummy variables are used to convert categorical variables (such as gender, industry type, job type, etc) so that they can be used in multiple regression analyses. Dummy variables typically take the form of (0, 1) variables or on/off variables. For example, we could turn gender into a dummy variable by coding male as 1 and female as 0, or vice versa.

Table A2 | Construction of measures used in the analysis of change in employment status in Chapter 3

Variable name	Variable type	Description
CHANGE IN EMPLOYMENT STATUS		
Unemployed	Dummy	Respondents were asked whether they were currently in full-time or part-time employment, or were unemployed (unemployed = 1, otherwise = 0). Unemployed respondents were subsequently asked whether they chose or were forced to leave.
Left organisation	Dummy	Refers to those respondents who had either voluntarily left their job and were currently unemployed, or respondents who had voluntarily moved to another organisation.
Changed job	Dummy	Respondents were asked whether they were doing the same job or a different job to the one they were doing last year. Two response categories were provided, 'same' (coded 0) and 'different' (coded 1).

Table A3 | Construction of measures used in the analysis of organisational and job content change in Chapter 4

Variable name	Variable type	Description
ORGANISATIONAL CHANGE/JOB CONTENT CHANGE		
Type of organisational change	Dummy	Respondents were asked whether their organisation had been involved in any type of change programme in the previous year; if yes, had it involved any of the following: redundancies, restructuring, mergers or acquisitions, introduced new technologies, reorganisation of their work, and/or culture change. All items were yes/no response format.
Amount of organisational change	Dummy	A count was made across the six items measuring the type of organisational change. This count was then converted into dummy variables reflecting low (1 change), moderate (2–3 changes) or high (4+) organisational change. (The count measure was converted to dummy variables because of its skewed distribution.)
Workplace change	Interval	Respondents were asked across 11 items whether there had been any change at their workplace compared with last year, and how substantial the change had been. The items are presented in the main body of the text. Three factors emerged: job design (6 items, Alpha = 0.76), new technology (3 items, Alpha = 0.64), and deal alterations (2 items, Alpha = 0.34).
Job content change	Dummy	Respondents were asked whether their job content or the way he or she did it had changed in any way during the past year (yes = 1, otherwise = 0). If 'yes', respondents were required to report the main way their job had changed, using an open response format. Responses were categorised using a coding frame developed by the researchers.
Personnel policy change	Dummy	Respondents were asked whether there had been any changes in the past year in the organisation's personnel policies and practices. If 'yes', four follow-up questions were asked to ascertain which policies had changed. All items were yes/no response format.
Attitudes to change at work	Interval	Seven items were used to measure respondents' attitudes towards change at work (eg 'There is too much change going on in the place where I work.'). The items are presented in the main body of the text. Factor analysis revealed no useful groupings.

Table A4 | Construction of measures used in the analysis of violations of psychological contract in Chapter 5

Variable name	Variable type	Description
Organisational violation	Dummy	Respondents were asked whether the organisation had broken any promises or commitments to them in the last year that they felt to be particularly important. If 'yes', respondents were asked about the content of the promise (eg pay), who had broken the promise (eg line manager), their attributions as to why the promise had been broken (eg due to the other party's incompetence, whether the other party was personally responsible, whether the other party had acted deliberately) and to what extent they had experienced certain emotions following the incident (eg anger).
Employee violation	Interval	12 items were used to measure various aspects of employee violation (eg 'Criticised your boss behind his/her back'). The items, factor analysis results, and Alpha reliabilities are reported in the main text

Notes on statistical procedures

1 Reliability of variables

Cronbach's Alpha coefficient, the most popular test of inter-item consistency reliability, was used to assess the reliability of variables. The Alpha coefficient is considered to represent good internal consistency when the coefficient is above 0.8, acceptable in the 0.7 range and less than satisfactory when below 0.6.

2 Path analysis

The figures in the report are a summary of standard multiple regressions using SPSS for Windows, Version 8. The numbers displayed in boxes lying on the lines running from left to right represent the beta weights (standardised regression coefficients) from the regression analysis. A 'slightly significant' beta weight ('†') has an associated p-value less than 0.10, a 'significant' beta weight ('*') has an associated p-value less than 0.05, a 'strongly significant' beta weight ('**') has an associated p-value less than 0.01, and a 'very strongly significant' beta weight ('***') has an associated p-value less than 0.001. The boxes with arrows going into them are the dependent variables in the regression run.
Panel regression analyses were used to assess the extent of change in dependent variables. The analysis of change in 1999 measures of dependent variables is achieved by the inclusion of the dependent variable in 1998 as an independent variable. For more information on causal analysis of panel data see Finkel.[1]

The labels beneath the dependent variables ('Adj Rsq') indicates the adjusted R-square. The adjusted R-square provides a more conservative estimate of the amount of variance that is explained in the dependent variable by the independent variables. The number of independent variables associated with the regression equation inflates the magnitude of the unadjusted R-square, hence the adjusted R-square corrects for this by taking into account the number of independent variables. The value for the adjusted R-square presented in the figures has been discounted to remove the contribution to explanation of the 1998 measure of the dependent variable, since to include this would make the adjusted R-square misleading as an index of the extent to which the independent variables explain change in the dependent variable.

3 Discriminant and logistic analyses

Discriminant and logistic analyses were performed in cases where the dependent variable was a categorical variable.

1. Finkel S.E. (1995) *Causal Analysis with Panel Data*. Thousand Oaks, Calif, Sage.

Appendix 3

Zero-order correlations for sector, antecedents, the psychological contract and outcome variables for 1999 measures (n=493)

	1	2	3	4	5	6	7	8	9	10	11	12	13	14
1. HR practices	1.00													
2. Direct participation	.23	1.00												
3. Psychological contract	.37	.22	1.00											
4. Commitment	.28	.20	.58	1.00										
5. Life satisfaction	.14	.18	.37	.33	1.00									
6. Work satisfaction	.21	.20	.56	.54	.73	1.00								
7. Employment relations	.24	.05	.56	.42	.32	.45	1.00							
8. Security	.19	.10	.39	.24	.19	.26	.27	1.00						
9. Motivation	.22	.18	.54	.53	.49	.69	.43	.26	1.00					
10. Effort	.05	−.06	.05	.18	.12	.23	.13	.02	.26	1.00				
11. Intention to quit	−.21	−.16	−.42	−.39	−.36	−.47	−.29	−.24	−.41	−.09	1.00			
12. Citizenship behaviour	.04	.23	.16	.37	.09	.21	.10	.04	.23	.17	−.10	1.00		
13. Innovative behaviour	.25	.32	.09	.20	.08	.06	.06	.07	.21	.15	−.10	.22	1.00	
14. Performance (self-rating)	.18	.14	.17	.21	.15	.24	.11	.08	.21	.18	−.10	.12	.16	1.00

Note

Correlations above: 0.09 are significant at the 5% level; 0.12 are significant at the 1% level; 0.15 are significant at the 0.1% level.